INTENTIONAL BEHAVIOR
AND
MOTIVATION

A Cognitive Theory

THE LIPPINCOTT COLLEGE PSYCHOLOGY SERIES

Under the Editorship of

Carl P. Duncan, Northwestern University

and Julius Wishner, University of Pennsylvania

INTENTIONAL BEHAVIOR
AND
MOTIVATION

A Cognitive Theory

FRANCIS W. IRWIN

University of Pennsylvania

J. B. LIPPINCOTT COMPANY

Philadelphia   ●   New York   ●   Toronto

To the memory of
Francis B. Irwin
and
Caroline S. Irwin,
my father and mother

Editor's Foreword

The author of this volume, Professor Francis W. Irwin, has been a contributor to experimental and theoretical psychology for almost forty years. For eight years he edited the *Journal of Experimental Psychology*; and he has served the psychological profession as consulting editor of a number of its most important journals. Those of us who have had the good fortune to be associated with him over some of these years have been immensely enriched by his disciplined thinking and teaching and have urged him to bring his insights together in a single work for the benefit of his colleagues and the profession. This book will meet the needs of the field for a disciplined, yet not impoverished, approach to the study of motivation.

The unifying thread of Professor Irwin's work has been concern with the problems of motivation: preferences, desires, aversions, intentions, choice-behavior, decision-making. To understand the development of these themes fully, it is advantageous to see them in the context of his understanding of related fields, *e.g.,* epistemology and philosophy of science, and his continuing commitment to the scientific study of behavior. In this book, Professor Irwin delineates not only a theory of intentional behavior, but also, particularly for the sensitive reader, a sophisticated view of the possibilities of a truly scientific psychology. He strives for precision in conceptualization while remaining skeptical of premature quantification. He insists on objective investigation but leaves ample scope for the complexity of motivation observed in higher organisms. He espouses a cognitive approach, conceiving of acts as reflective of expectancies, but does not leave the organism "immersed in thought." In all these ways, this volume may be regarded as the embodiment of the program for the study of motivation set forth in Tolman's *Purposive behavior in animals and men.* Although Professor

Irwin's modesty leads him to call his theory "neo-Tolmanian," his own contributions are so much the bulk of the current volume that it would appear to warrant the label "Irwinian."

This book could serve to good effect as the basic or adjunct text for courses on motivation beyond the introductory course in psychology. It will require serious effort on the part of the student, but with rich rewards in the offing.

The greater part of professional psychologists must certainly be included in the potential audience for this book, but a great many others can profit from careful study of it. For example, students of theory of knowledge and ethics will find Professor Irwin's formulation of the criteria of discrimination, preference, and intention instructive. Similarly, students of that part of jurisprudence concerned with problems of responsibility for behavior, students of those areas of economics and political science in which preferences, choices, and biases are important, along with students of all areas touched by problems of motivation will find a great deal of interest and use in this work.

If the reader has detected a special note of pride in these prefatory remarks, he is not mistaken; the pride is in being the instrumentality whereby this long-awaited work is now being presented. The editors and publisher believe that there is a substantial probability that this book will come to be recognized as a major contribution to the science of psychology.

Philadelphia
July, 1970

Julius Wishner
For the Consulting Editors

Preface

The set of interrelated concepts presented in this book developed over the course of several decades of teaching undergraduate and graduate courses in motivation and conducting research on human choice-behavior. An early stage was represented by an attempt to clarify the concept of "volition" as it has been used in experimental psychology (Irwin, 1942); then, after an extended attempt to bring together in harmony the concepts of Lewin and Tolman, the notions began to settle into their present form as indicated by articles on discrimination and preference (1958), desire and aversion (1961), and expectancy (1966). During most of this time I contemplated nothing so pretentious as a psychological system or even a significant fragment of one; what eventually emerged, including especially the close interrelations among the defining criteria for motivational and cognitive concepts, was surprising to me, although it might not have been so to others. I had aimed only to make clear to my students and myself a few ideas that might capture the sense of human and animal motivational phenomena as I saw them and yet be firmly linked to the data of psychology as an experimental science. This bit of personal history may help to account for the direction this book has taken and for various limitations of its scope.

The scheme as presented is at an intermediate level of formalization. Although it may be too formal for the taste of some and too informal for that of others, it has benefitted from tests of discussion with serious students of psychology at all levels from that of undergraduates to that of professionals in the field. The conceptual analysis is qualitative, rather than quantitative. Although not everyone will agree with me, I believe that the discordant fragmentation of contemporary psychological theory reflects an insufficient concern for the qualitative properties of the concepts that are employed, as well as a hope, scarcely justified by the present scene, that quantitative or quasiquantitative elaboration of almost any kind of data will somehow provide us with a clear and unified science—if not now, then at some happy future time.

My intellectual debts are more than I know how to repay. Deepest of all are those to the late Edgar A. Singer, Jr., philosopher, and Edward C. Tolman and Kurt Lewin, psychologists, not only for their ideas and the influence of their luminous minds but also for their friendship and kindnesses to me. I am grateful to many colleagues and students who have aided me by discussion, suggestions, criticism of drafts and manuscripts in all stages of preparation, and not least, by encouragement. In particular, informal conversations with Eugene Galanter, R. Duncan Luce, and Jacob Beck were more valuable than they could have known. David H. Krantz read the whole of a late draft, much to its advantage, after having already helped me over difficult ground at several earlier stages. Richard L. Solomon suggested many improvements, especially in illustrations and applications. Thomas S. Wallsten, Burton S. Rosner, and Ching-Yuan Chiang also made helpful comments. That the book was accomplished at all is due to Julius Wishner, partly in his editorial capacity but most of all as a friend and colleague who made me believe that it was worth doing. The faults in it are my own.

I wish also to thank Miss Terri Forlano for her expert and patient manufacture of numerous drafts of the text, figures, and tables, and James K. Winston, Jr., for assistance with the references, indexes, and proofs.

I gratefully acknowledge the permission of Robert Leeper, the American Psychological Association, Inc., and The Journal Press to reproduce schematically the material in Fig. 9.1, and of Curtis Brown, Ltd. to quote from a novel by Miss Ivy Compton-Burnett.

Preparation of this book was greatly aided by Grant MH-06580 to the author from the National Institute of Mental Health.

Philadelphia   Francis W. Irwin
June, 1970

Contents

Part II

Some Problems, Applications, and Extensions of the System

PART I

Introduction to a
Situation-Act-Outcome Psychology

1

Introduction

AN ILLUSTRATION

In an episode of "Bullivant and the Lambs," by Ivy Compton-Burnett,* two young boys are found building a hutch in the garden of an English country estate. Their father comes by, exchanges a few words with them, and proceeds on his walk. As they had expected, he takes a path that will lead him to a bridge over a deep ravine; and they had earlier learned that this bridge was so weakened by a storm the previous night that it would not bear a man's weight, although the damage is not readily visible. It happens that a sign has been posted and his life is spared, but only at the cost of his later discovering that the children had known of his danger when he passed them. Instantly he draws the conclusion already drawn by the reader and, confronting the boys before their mother and other members of the family, he grimly says, "My children desire my death."

THE ILLUSTRATION INTERPRETED

Taken as if it were a fragment of history rather than of fiction, and freely analyzed for much that the author's artistry leaves to the reader's imagination, this incident illustrates the main elements of the psychological system that is to be set forth in the ensuing chapters. It may be useful to consider these elements briefly and informally in the context of the illustration before attempting to define and discuss them more rigorously and show their relations to experimental facts. In the process a number of terms will be used that will later assume technical status; these will be

*This remarkable novel was published in 1949 by Alfred A. Knopf, Inc., New York. It was originally published in 1947 by Victor Gollancz, Ltd., London, under the title, "Manservant and Maidservant."

listed in the section-headings and italicized on their first appearance in the text.

As will be seen, the system rests upon three undefined or primitive concepts, those of situations, acts, and outcomes. It will therefore be called a "situation-act-outcome," or "SAO," psychology.

Act, Intentional Act, Chosen Act, Alternative Act, Act of Abstention

The behavior that we wish to understand is the children's *act* of abstaining from warning the father of the danger to his life. This act was committed by each of the children, whatever support each may have had from the presence of the other and whether or not either would have committed the act in the absence of the other. Furthermore, it was an *intentional act, chosen* over the *alternative act* of giving warning. Although the novelist and the reader must share unstated assumptions at various points, these claims are well grounded in the novel and would probably have been accepted in the ordinary senses of the terms by the father and the children. Indeed, the whole remaining course of the story depends upon some such understanding.

The children could have warned their father but they intentionally did not do so. Thus, they performed an *act of abstention* from the alternative act of giving warning. This is by no means equivalent to the mere nonoccurrence of the alternative act, and the manner in which both the characters and the reader react to it testifies to its status as a definite act in its own right. No doubt its very invisibility, coupled with its diagnostic significance for the relations between the children and their father, is responsible for its seeming even more horrifying than various acts of incest, suicide, pretended suicide, and murder that are encountered in other novels by the same author. In one sense, the children do nothing at all; in another, they attempt patricide. The distinction is clear enough if one considers what would have been the case had the children not learned about the danger—then, too, they would not have given warning, but neither would they have intentionally refrained from doing so.

Outcome, Act-Outcome Expectancy, Expected Outcome

To continue the informal analysis of the illustration, it is supposed that the children's behavior depended upon both cognitive and motivational factors. Let us consider first the cognitive factors, which include discriminations, perceptions, knowledge, beliefs, expectancies, and the like. Among these, we focus particularly upon certain expectancies, and assert that the chosen act depended critically upon what the children expected would be the *outcomes* of the alternative acts between which they chose. The general nature of these expectancies is clear: the children expected that their father would continue to live if they warned him rather than abstained from warning him, and they expected that he would die if they abstained from warning him rather than giving him warning. Expectancies that relate a pair of alternative acts to an outcome in this way, so that the one act is seen as more likely than the other to have the outcome, are called *act-outcome expectancies.*

That the children had such act-outcome expectancies is a conclusion drawn from what the novelist has told us about them and their history. The argument for this conclusion might take the following form: the children are perceptive and intelligent, they know their father's habits, they see him in the course of carrying out such a habit, and they had heard of the damage to the bridge; but any sufficiently perceptive and intelligent person who knew the father this well, who saw him under these conditions, and knew about the bridge would have the expectancies that we have attributed to the children; therefore, the children must have had these expectancies. The argument takes much for granted. It employs poorly defined psychological terms—"perceptive," "intelligent," "know"— and makes an implicit assumption that there are laws relating such traits and processes to the formation of expectancies. For our present purposes, however, it is the conclusion itself, not the means by which it was arrived at, that is important; what matters for the illustration is that the children have these expectancies, as the author clearly wishes us to believe.

Since an act-outcome expectancy relates an outcome to a pair of alternative acts, it will be useful to have a name for this outcome, and it will be called the *expected outcome* of that act of the pair that is seen as the more likely to produce it. The children see their father's death as more likely if they abstain from warning him than if they warn him; hence, his death is the expected outcome of abstention. Similarly, his continued existence is the expected outcome of giving warning. Thus, the children not only chose one act over another but at the same time they chose the expected outcome of one act over the expected outcome of the other. We take it to be true that every choice is a choice both of an act and of an expected outcome. It goes without saying that the actual outcome of an act need not coincide with the expected outcome, as indeed it did not in this case—the father lived, although the children expected him to die.

Situation, Common Prior Field, Discriminanda, Discrimination

An act takes place at a particular time, in a particular place, and under particular circumstances of the actor and his environment. In the illustration the time is during the early years of the present century, and the place is in England. The immediate physical environment, as it might be represented in a stage setting, is the grounds in front of a country house. The circumstances of the actors, *i.e.*, the children, include the facts that they are playing together, that they know their father's habits, and that they know that the bridge over which he may be expected to pass is dangerous. All of these physical, social, and psychological facts constitute features of the *situation* in which the children acted.

Besides this, the father becomes part of the situation for the time of his brief appearance; and it is during this time that the children commit their act. Let us call that part of the situation that existed just before the father appeared on the scene the *common prior field*. If this were an experiment, we could introduce whatever changes we pleased into this common field—we could have the father's entrance as one condition, but we could substitute for this the entrance of the mother or of some other member of the family; or we could have one of the children absent and see how the remaining one behaved if the father appeared; and so on, indefinitely. What we chose to do would depend upon what we wanted to find out. In any case, whatever we added to the common prior field could be called a *discriminandum,* to use Tolman's term, and we would wish to compare the children's behavior in situations that were the same except for the discriminanda that were present. If they were found to display different intentional acts in two such situations, they would be said to *discriminate* between the discriminanda that were presented for comparison.

Preference, Common Outcome Field, Differential Outcomes, Preferred and Dispreferred Outcomes, Indifference

Turning now to the motivation of the children's act, we assert that, however complex its antecedents and concomitants, it expressed itself as a *preference* for one of the two expected outcomes over the other. Whichever way the choice fell, much would remain the same—the children themselves and the rest of their family would still be alive, their home would still be there, and the more remote world would be largely unaffected; we can call those circumstances that remain the same, regardless of the choice, the *common outcome field*. But the expected outcomes of the two acts are very different; in the one case, the father is alive, in the other he is dead. We shall call these the *differential outcomes* of the two acts. A choice, then, expresses a preference for one of a pair of differential outcomes over the other, in some common outcome field. The outcome that is chosen will be called the *preferred outcome* and the other member of the pair, the *dispreferred outcome*. If neither differential outcome of a pair is preferred to the other, the organism (person or animal) will be said to be *indifferent* between these outcomes.

Affective Zero, Desire, Aversion, Neutrality

Both laymen and psychologists speak of differential outcomes as being pleasant or unpleasant, satisfying or unsatisfying, rewarding or punishing, or the like. To distinguish among outcomes that correspond to the positive and negative members of these pairs of adjectives we need an *affective zero;* this, to put it roughly, is the preference value of an outcome such that the person or animal does not care whether it happens or not. Any outcome preferred to the affective zero will be said to be *desired,* and any outcome dispreferred to the affective zero will be called *aversive;* the corresponding states of preference will be called *desire* and *aversion.* If an organism is indifferent between some outcome and the affective zero, that outcome will be called *neutral* and the organism's state will be said to be one of *neutrality* toward the outcome.

It will be recalled that the father in our original illustration concluded that his children "desired" his death. This is equivalent to saying that they preferred a future without him to one in which he figured; taken strictly, it is an assertion that they preferred his death to the affective zero. This judgment, although perhaps oversimplified, appears to be at least part of what Miss Compton-Burnett wished her readers to understand.

Interlocked Triad, Intentional Act, Intended Outcome

According to the above analysis, the children's act depended upon three psychological states: (1) a preference for their father's death over his continued existence, (2) an expectancy that this act, rather than its alternative, would lead to the preferred outcome, and (3) an expectancy that the alternative act rather than this act would lead to the dispreferred outcome. A preference and pair of act-outcome expectancies that are interrelated in this way are called an *interlocked triad.* As can be seen, in such a triad the expected outcome in one expectancy is the preferred outcome in the preference, and the expected outcome in the other expectancy is the dispreferred outcome in the preference.

We return now to the notion of intentional acts, which was introduced above. An act will be called *intentional,* by definition, if and only if its occurrence depends upon the presence of an interlocked triad such that (1) the act in question is a member of the pair of the alternative acts in each of the two expectancies of the triad and (2) the expected outcome of the act is the preferred outcome in the preference of the triad. These conditions are met in the illustration as we have interpreted it. The father's death is both the expected outcome of the act of refraining from warning him and the preferred member of the pair of differential outcomes. From this it becomes a natural step to define the *intended outcome* of an act as the expected and preferred outcome of that act. The father's death, then, was the outcome that the children intended by their act.

Chosen Act, Chosen Outcome

In trying to discover what can be meant by saying that the children's behavior constituted an intentional act, it has been necessary to mention frequently the alternative act, which they did not commit. Moreover, the interlocked triad upon which their act depended refers to each act exactly twice, once in each expectancy. According to this, whenever an act is intentional, it is related by an interlocked triad to some alternative act, the expected outcome of which is the dispreferred outcome of the preference in the triad. Thus, if an intentional act occurs, it is a *chosen act* and its expected outcome is a *chosen outcome.* In performing their act of abstaining from warning their father, the children chose both this act and its expected outcome of his death over the act of warning him and its expected outcome of his continued existence.

A Diagnostic Rule

Perhaps the most effective feature of the illustration in its place in the novel is the sudden and chilling insight into the children's motivation that their act induces. Although the father is pictured as meanly despotic and it is clear that his relations with his children are unhappy, it is not until they knowingly let the father go to what they expect will be his death that the reader perceives the depth of their disaffection.

If the reader were asked on what grounds he has concluded that the children desired their father's death, he might reply that the children *must* have had this desire, since they intentionally refrained from warning him of his danger when they expected that this would lead to his death, whereas they equally expected that if they were to warn him, his life would be saved. But such an argument, if generalized, amounts to saying that *if an act is intentional and its occurrence depends upon a pair of act-outcome expectancies, then it also depends upon a preference for its expected outcome over the expected outcome of the alternative act.*

This statement will be called a *diagnostic rule,* because it enables one to draw inferences about the motivation of intentional acts from their cognitive determiners. Whether there is an inverse rule that permits the diagnosis of the cognitions involved in intentional acts from knowledge of the motivation of these acts will be discussed later. At this stage, however, it is important to note that the rule as stated above comes to this: if an intentional act depends upon a pair of complementary act-outcome expectancies, then it also depends upon that preference which, together with these expectancies, constitutes an interlocked triad. It will be shown later (Chapter 7) that this rule is not derivable merely from the definition of intentional acts, but goes beyond the definition.

SUMMARY

Fig. 1.1 represents most of the concepts introduced in this chapter and their relations to each other, although a few concepts have been omitted from the figure in order to make the systematic skeleton more visible. The basic or undefined concepts appear at the foot of the figure; concepts at higher levels depend definitionally upon those below, as shown by connecting lines.

The basic concepts are situation, act, and outcome. A situation includes all of the circumstances of an organism prior to an act, including its physical and social environment and its psychological and physiological states. If an organism's behavior is observed in two different situations, these will have some features in common, the common prior field, and will differ from each other in one or more features, the discriminanda. Similarly, the circumstances of an organism after it has acted constitute the outcome of its act. If two outcomes are compared, they will have

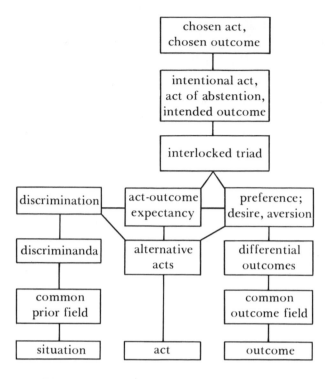

Fig. 1.1. Principal concepts introduced in Chapter 1

Connections between boxes at different levels indicate definitional dependence of concepts at higher levels upon those at lower levels. Horizontal connections indicate relations between empirical criteria as discussed in Chapters 3 and 5.

some features in common, the common outcome field, and one or more features that are different, the differential outcomes. Whatever an organism may be said to do is an act; alternative acts are those that cannot be performed simultaneously. (Situations, acts, and outcomes are discussed in Chapter 2.)

If an organism behaves differently in two situations and if this difference in behavior depends upon the differential outcomes of its acts, it will be said to discriminate between the discriminanda and to prefer one of the two differential outcomes over the other. (Chapter 3)

A differential outcome that is preferred to the affective zero is said to be desired and one that is dispreferred to the affective zero is said to be aversive; if an organism is indifferent between the affective zero and some differential outcome, the latter is called neutral. (Chapter 4)

An organism that treats one of two alternative acts as more likely than the other to have a particular differential outcome is said to exhibit an act-outcome expectancy that relates that outcome to the two acts. The outcome is called the expected outcome of the act that is seen as the more likely to be followed by it. (Chapter 5).

An interlocked triad is made up of a preference and a pair of act-outcome expectancies such that the preferred outcome in the preference is the expected outcome of one of the alternative acts in the expectancies and the dispreferred outcome is the expected outcome of the other alternative act in the expectancies. An intentional act is an act whose occurrence depends upon the existence of an interlocked triad, and the expected outcome of an intentional act is called an intended outcome. If an intentional act occurs, it and its expected outcome are called, respectively, a chosen act and a chosen outcome. (Chapter 6)

A diagnostic rule enables a preference to be diagnosed from knowledge of the pair of act-outcome expectancies upon which the occurrence of an intentional act depends. (Chapter 7)

NOTES AND COMMENTS

1. Two departures from common usage need to be acknowledged. First, the term "dispreferred," for which no dictionary sanction seems to exist, has been introduced. It is sometimes badly needed. If o is preferred to o', o' is often called the "less preferred" outcome, but this is like saying that the smaller of two objects is the "less larger." Second, recent usage among psychologists permits one to write that an object is aversive to a subject when, by dictionary rules, one should write that the subject is averse (or aversive) to the object. If, for example, it were necessary to say that a subject was aversive to an experimenter, there would indeed be ambiguity—one would not know who disliked whom; but such statements will be avoided.

2. It is worth noting that the concept of intended outcome as introduced here is one of the various meanings of the common notion of the "purpose" of an act.

2

Situations, Acts, and Outcomes

Because *situation, act,* and *outcome* are to play the role of basic terms in an SAO system, they require illustration and comment rather than definition. Their use will clarify their meaning.

SITUATIONS

In a psychological experiment the object of observation is something that an organism does during some interval of time in some set of circumstances (*cf.* Skinner, 1938, p. 6). These circumstances taken together are called a *situation,* and include the physical and social environment of the organism and its own psychological and physiological properties and states prior to an act. No one supposes that all describable aspects of a situation are equally important, but what is and what is not important depends in the short run upon the observer's purposes and in the long run upon the progress of the science. The discovery that one thing matters and another does not is what makes the observations worth while.

A situation must be describable but the description obviously cannot be complete. An experimental article may tell us too little about the conditions of the experiment, but whatever of this sort it does tell us is a description of the situations of the experiment. Especially critical is a description of the ways in which experimental situations are alike and are different, *i.e.,* the constant features and the "independent variables." But however careful a psychologist may be, he knows like any other experimental scientist that he runs the risk of being shown later that he has omitted exactly what was most important from his description of the situations in his experiment.

The fact that features of the organism itself constitute aspects of the situation must not be overlooked. To interpret an act, one may need to know the species of the subjects, their age, their sex, their intelligence, their states of nutrition, their emotional state, their states of expectancy or preference, etc. In the case of the children in Chapter 1, we needed to know that they had overheard the conversation about the bridge not only to interpret their abstaining from warning their father but even to know that this behavior had occurred. Equally important aspects of the situation were the facts that they knew their father's habits and that they were sufficiently intelligent and perceptive to foresee the probable consequences of the alternative acts that were available to them.

In stimulus-response psychology, much of what we have called a situation would be treated as a stimulus or a complex of stimuli. This is reasonably clear, at any rate, for those aspects of a situation that lie outside the organism's skin. It is perhaps arguable with respect to those aspects of the situation that are states of the organism, although even here the pressures toward conceptualizing such states as stimuli can easily be seen. As examples, observe how Bolles (1967) seems to be driven by an S—R attitude toward conceiving of motivation as stimuli; and consider the elaborate stimulus-sets that Estes (1958) has proposed to substitute for the concept of drive. Three things tend to result from such pressure, none of which is desirable: the word "stimulus," useful for designating energies operating upon receptors or neural structures, becomes roughly equivalent to our term "situation" and lends a specious air of precision to a vague notion; or it is unguardedly assumed that even the most complex situations and objects are in principle reducible to congeries of simple stimulus energies; or hands are thrown up and stimuli become hypothetical and ghostly. The reader must judge in the end whether the present strategy of assigning the responsibility for describing particular situations to the experimenter or the interpreter of an experiment evades these difficulties without introducing others that are equally repugnant. When stimuli are referred to here, they will always be parts of situations, but it will not be assumed that "[a] situation is, of course, upon final analysis, resolvable into a complex group of stimuli" (Watson, 1924, p. 10). It is doubtful that Watson himself made serious use of this assumption.

Common Prior Fields and Discriminanda

Whenever it is desired to compare the behavior of an organism in one situation with that in another, the two situations will necessarily differ in

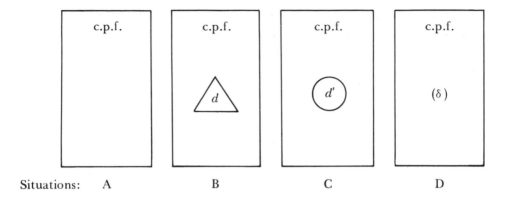

Situations: A   B   C   D

Fig. 2.1. Common prior field and discriminanda

In Situation A the c.p.f. is alone; in B it contains the discriminandum d; in C it contains the discriminandum d'; in D it contains the null discriminandum, δ. To test for discrimination between d and d' one would use Situations B and C. To test for detection of d (i.e., discrimination between d and δ) one would use Situations B and D; this would be the same as using B and A, since A and D are identical by the definition of δ.

some ways and have some things in common. Putting it roughly, the *common prior field* (c.p.f.) is made up of what is in common and the *discriminanda* (d and d') are those parts of the situations that are different between them. (See Fig. 2.1.) This is imprecise because, although all of the differences between two situations can be assigned to d and d', not all of the common features can be assigned to the c.p.f. without performing the impossible feat of finding discriminanda that have nothing whatever in common. Two colors that differ in hue, brightness, and saturation are both colors, at any rate, not to mention their spatial extension, temporal duration, etc. A large and a small sunflower seed presented to a rat for choice are complex objects but enough alike to be called sunflower seeds. The point hardly needs pressing. What it comes to is this: (1) it is well to include all differences between situations in the discriminanda, since otherwise differences in behavior in the different situations may be ascribed to the wrong aspects of the situations, but (2) the experimenter must be permitted to include in the discriminanda as much as he wishes of what the situations have in common. As to (1), if two situations differ in some respect that is *known* not to matter for the behavior, then it is irrelevant how this respect is classified. If astrology is false, one need not report variations in the signs of the zodiac under which the work was

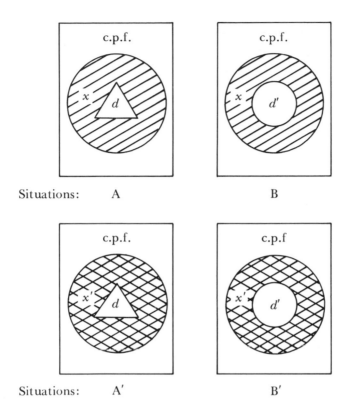

Fig. 2.2 Variation of a parameter in a discrimination experiment

Situations A and B are used to test for discrimination between d and d' in a c.p.f. that contains x, which is some value of a parametric variable. Situations A' and B' are used to test for discrimination between the same discriminanda, d and d', in the same c.p.f. with x', a different value of the parameter, substituted for x.

done, much less take the pains to distribute these signs among the discriminanda. As to (2), what commonly happens in experiments on discrimination is that the experimenter chooses in advance some convenient c.p.f. and then adds to it sometimes d and sometimes d', these discriminanda having been selected with great care for both their likenesses and their differences. In Fig. 2.1, for example, the c.p.f. is represented by Situation A, the same c.p.f. with d added to it by Situation B, and the same c.p.f. with d' added to it by Situation C. If two color patches are intended to differ only in hue, and therefore to be alike in size, shape, brightness, and saturation, the experimenter may decide whether to regard the size, shape, etc., as part of the c.p.f. or as part of the discriminanda. The decision will rest partly upon convention and partly upon the state of relevant knowledge and theory.

To carry the last point further, one can see that the discrimination between two hues may be affected by the size of the color patches, their shape, their temporal duration, the location of their retinal images, the subject's state of adaptation, and the like. Such variables are then "parameters" of hue discrimination. This is represented in Fig. 2.2. In this figure, Situations A and B could be used to test for discrimination between the discriminanda d and d', and the same is true of Situations A' and B'. The difference between the two pairs of situations lies in the introduction of a parameter with the value x into A and B and with the value x' into A' and B'. So, for example, if d and d' are two different color patches, x might represent one size of patch and x' a different size.

What an experimenter reports about the c.p.f. depends largely upon his views as to what are and what are not parameters of the process he is studying, aside from matters having to do with apparatus and procedures that are required for the observations. In work on hue discrimination, it is not usual to report, or even to control, human subjects' states of food deprivation. But in studying taste, if hunger affects taste sensitivity, this state will presumably be controlled and reported.[1] * Again, a subject's membership in ADA or the John Birch Society might not concern a student of hue or taste discrimination but it could hardly be overlooked by a social psychologist in research on political behavior.

The Null Discriminandum (δ)

In some cases, one compares an organism's behavior in a situation made up of some c.p.f. plus some discriminandum, d, with its behavior in a situation made up of the same c.p.f. plus another discriminandum, d', where d and d' are both positive objects of some sort, like color patches. In other cases, however, the comparison is between two situations of which one is a c.p.f. plus some d and the other is the c.p.f. alone. In a *catch trial* in psychophysics, one holds the situation constant during a trial and introduces no stimulus; and in many experiments on learning and motivation in animals, one holds the situation constant except for periods

*Notes referred to by superior numbers will be found at the ends of the chapters under NOTES AND COMMENTS, which also include, however, some remarks of a general character that are not cited in the main body of the text.

during which a signal, such as a buzzer or flashing light, is turned on, the outcome to the animal of its behavior being different in the presence of the signal (the "discriminative stimulus," in Skinner's language) than in its absence. It is awkward and imprecise to speak of an animal's response to the *absence* of a signal; if a rat in a Skinner box presses a bar when a given signal is not on, and is said to be responding to the absence of the flashing light, why not also say that it is responding to the absence of, say, a rattlesnake? The light and the snake are equally absent.

To keep such cases straight it is useful to define the *null discriminandum* (δ) as that which, when added to a c.p.f., leaves the c.p.f. unaltered. Thus, one may write, "(c.p.f., δ) = c.p.f.," where the comma within the parentheses represents what is meant when one says that a discriminandum is *added to* a c.p.f. In Fig. 2.1, Situation A (c.p.f. alone) is identical to Situation D (c.p.f. plus δ). Then discriminations between situations with and without some positive discriminandum become discriminations between (c.p.f., d) and (c.p.f., δ), with c.p.f. constant.

ACTS

Anything that an organism can be said to do is an *act*. No advantage is gained by fixing clear boundaries for this concept; wherever they are placed, the enclosed region will be too narrow or too broad to please psychologists in general. The risk of being too broad will be taken here—as was said in Chapter 1, it is not hard to ignore uninteresting cases. The writer once suggested (Irwin, 1958) that anything that is to qualify as an act must be ascribable in part to processes within the body of the organism, so that jumping from a window would be an act but the ensuing free fall would not. Although this would probably include everything that is familiar in the literature, it seems well to leave the question open, perhaps even to the point of relaxing the requirement concerning living organisms and letting computers perform acts if they so desire.

Interesting, although technically difficult, candidates for status as acts are paying attention to what someone is saying, recalling the name of the capital of Idaho, trying to forget having called one friend by the name of another, and the like. Acts are not in general defined psychologically, but this does not exclude psychologically defined acts if it turns out to be desirable to include them. If, however, they are to be counted, we must know how to identify them and their occurrences and nonoccurrences, which has not yet become easy to do. The present system regards the unsupported statements of human subjects about themselves as insufficient evidence for such acts.

It is common to count as an act anything that has a recordable effect, such as a rat's breaking a beam of light in a runway or operating a relay that signifies that a bar was pressed, and such acts will be accepted here. Causing an observer to put a rating mark or category name on a record sheet is such an act; the observer functions here as a mere instrument. Unhappily the precision and validity of observers as instruments are not always high, or even known.

It is not altogether flippant to say that an act is whatever obeys the same laws as other acts. For the purposes of psychology, acts must find their places in a systematic science of behavior. The emission of an alpha particle by a bit of uranium fails to qualify as an act for psychological purposes not so much because the uranium is conceived of as non-living as because, in spite of similarities between radioactive decay and "extinction," no one has found or expects to find, for example, that he can successfully reward or punish the uranium for such emission.

The word "response" will be used rarely in this book, on account of its S–R connotations. When it does occur, as in the term "differential response" (Chapter 3), the answer to the question, "Response to what?," will usually be clear.

Acts of Abstention

As was illustrated in Chapter 1, abstaining from committing some act, a, will be taken to be itself an act, always, indeed, an intentional act, and will be called an *act of abstention* (α_a); but there must be grounds for distinguishing these cases from mere failures of an act to occur. The reader may abstain from flying in an airplane but he cannot abstain from flying by flapping his arms. A card received from a book club reads: "To receive the monthly selection, do not return this card." Here, it matters to the subscriber, if not to the book club, whether he abstains from returning the card or merely forgets to do so; whichever happens, he receives the book, but in the first case he wants it and in the second he does not. Further clarification must await the discussion of intentional acts in Chapter 6.

Quantitative Properties of Acts

When acts have quantitative properties such as latencies, speeds, and amplitudes, they may be distinguished from each other thereby; but a latency, speed, or amplitude is a property of some act, not an act itself.[2]

The Molar-Molecular Dichotomy

The distinction between molar and molecular definitions of behavior was introduced into experimental psychology by Tolman (1932), who attributed it to C. D. Broad. In its variegated history it has acquired the value-connotations of a polemical term. For Tolman, purposiveness was an "emergent" property of behavior, and such properties were not, he thought, reducible to, or even capable of being inferred from, the properties of physical and physiological concomitants of them. Hull used the distinction somewhat differently, and contrasted "molar" with "neurological." At the same time, he thought of psychologists as working at different "degrees of the molar," and said (Hull, 1943, p. 21):

> In the end the work of all who differ only in this sense may find a place in a single systematic structure, the postulates or primary assumptions of those working at a more molar level ultimately appearing as theorems of those working at a more molecular level.

In the present system, acts are not defined either by emergent properties or as nonphysiological. On this question, as on many others, it seems wise to refrain from setting narrow boundaries for fundamental concepts and to relegate to the development of the science whatever sharpening is to be done. Acts as minute as action potentials from single nerve cells may be admitted together with acts as extensive as Beethoven's composition of his C-sharp minor quartet. The fact that it is easy to imagine the latter as involving (although not to our mind "made up of") a large number of smaller acts does not disqualify it. The question, not answerable in advance, is whether such an act makes sense in a science of behavior.

Occurrences of Acts

In later chapters it will frequently be necessary to have a symbol to denote the occurrence of a particular act. For this purpose, the symbol for the act will be printed in boldface type. Thus, "**a**" is to be read, "Act a occurs," or less precisely, "the occurrence of Act a."

OUTCOMES

The notion of *outcomes* is very similar to that of *situations*. Situations are the circumstances of an organism's environment, states, and properties at the time of an act or at some time prior to it; outcomes are the circumstances of the organism's environment, states, and properties at some time after an act.

Every act has a sequence of outcomes that reverberate indefinitely through time. This is not counter to common sense, which accepts history as the study of such reverberations of the acts of human beings singly and in groups. The psychologist, however, is normally interested only in those aspects of the outcomes of acts that affect the actor and his time scale is microscopic compared with the historian's. Indeed, so far as experiments are concerned, outcomes that fall beyond the intertrial interval create difficulties for him.

What does run against usage is to count as outcomes of an act even those aspects of the organism's circumstances after the act that are in no way contingent upon the act. It has become common enough, however, for special classes of outcomes such as rewards and punishments to be scheduled partially or wholly independent of an organism's acts; and, in any case, organisms do not distinguish perfectly between contingent and noncontingent outcomes of what they do, and are affected by both. As in the cases of situations and acts, nothing compels us to deal with outcomes that are irrelevant to our purposes. Further, as we saw in the illustration in Chapter 1, actual outcomes, whether contingent upon an act or not, do not invariably coincide with expected, preferred, or intended outcomes.

Perhaps the most dangerous, as well as the most frequent, failure of precision in dealing with outcomes is to treat them in isolation from the organism itself. To describe an outcome of a rat's having made the correct turn in a T-maze as "food" is concise but hardly psychological. "Being in the presence of a food pellet" is vague but tells us a little more; still, we may wonder whether the animal saw the pellet, smelled it, picked it up, chewed it, tasted it, swallowed it, digested it, and finally assimilated it, each of which outcomes of the correct turn may affect later acts. Similarly, "owning a picture" is an outcome of buying it; the question is open, however, whether once owned, it is hung and once hung, it is looked at. The dangers cannot be eliminated, since analysis must stop somewhere, and our own discussion will be subject to them; but it is true that the analysis of the outcomes of acts is too often stopped before it has properly begun. Much of the business of psychology has to do with discovering the effective outcomes of acts, that is, those that make a difference for future acts.

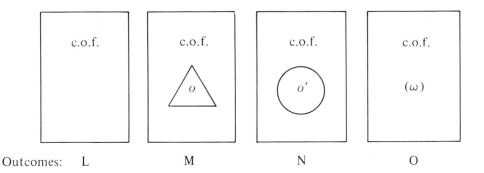

Outcomes: L   M   N   O

Fig. 2.3. Common outcome field and differential outcomes

In Outcome L the c.o.f. is alone; in M it
contains differential outcome o; in N it contains
differential outcome o'; in O it contains the null
differential outcome, ω. To test for preference
between o and o' one would use Outcomes M and
N. To test for the desiredness, aversiveness, or
neutrality of o (i.e., its preference relation to ω—cf.
Chapter 4) one would use Outcomes M and O; this
would be the same as using M and L, since L and O
are identical by the definition of ω.

Common Outcome Fields and Differential Outcomes

If an organism sometimes performs one act and sometimes another in
a given situation, the outcomes of the two acts will differ in some ways
and will have some things in common. In the parallel case of situations,
this kind of problem led us to distinguish between the common prior field
and the discriminanda, and a similar strategy is adopted here. The two
outcomes will be regarded as made up of a *common outcome field* (c.o.f.),
which is identical from one of the two situations to the other, and of
differential outcomes, o and o', which contain all the differences between
the outcomes. (See Fig. 2.3.) As was true in the case of discriminanda, the
differential outcomes are allowed to have some things in common, since it
is impossible to do otherwise. Again, as with d and d', the experimenter
usually first chooses some common field and then arranges affairs in such
a way that some o follows one act and some o' follows the other act, o
and o' having been carefully selected in the light of his purposes for both
their likenesses and their differences.

If one outcome involves an animal's obtaining two pellets of food
and the other involves its obtaining one pellet, it clearly depends upon
both data and theory whether it would be well to take o and o' as

containing two pellets and one, respectively, or whether to assign one pellet in each outcome to the c.o.f. and take o and o' to have one pellet and none. It will make no difference to the animal, but it will affect what is said about the animal's behavior. Similarly, if a person must choose between two positions that differ in salary, the preference value of the difference may be a function of the salary level that they have in common; according to most theories of the value of money, the difference in value between \$5,000 and \$10,000 per year is greater than that between \$100,000 and \$105,000.

This may remind the reader of what was said above about parameters in studies of discrimination—the salary level could be taken as a parameter that may affect the preference between a pair of differential outcomes. The audience before which behavior is carried out is often a significant parameter of the choice between acts and their expected outcomes—a choice that is made in one direction in public may be made in the opposite direction in private. A person who enjoys hearing a good orchestra play "The Stars and Stripes Forever" at an open-air summer concert may be contemptuous of the same music played by the same orchestra during its regular season. Knowledge of such contextual or parametric effects is often essential to correct interpretation of data concerning preferences.

Variation in a parameter that might affect a preference is represented in Fig. 2.4. Differential outcomes o and o' might be hearing "The Stars and Stripes Forever" and hearing the Brahms Symphony Number 1, respectively. Outcomes M and N include the condition (y) of hearing the music at an open-air concert, as contrasted with M' and N', which include the condition (y') of hearing the same music indoors at a regular-season concert. It is conceivable that o would be preferred to o' if the parameter had the value y and that o' would be preferred to o if the parameter had the value y', that is, that the Sousa would be preferred to the Brahms in the open air and the Brahms to the Sousa indoors.

The Null Differential Outcome (ω)

If one act leads to a c.o.f. plus some distinct outcome, o, whereas the other act leads simply to the c.o.f. itself, we shall speak of the second outcome as being made up of the c.o.f. plus the *null differential outcome*, ω. Thus, the comparison is between (c.o.f., o) and (c.o.f., ω), where ω is defined as that which, if added to an outcome, leaves the outcome unaltered. Parallel to the treatment of the null discriminandum, δ, we may

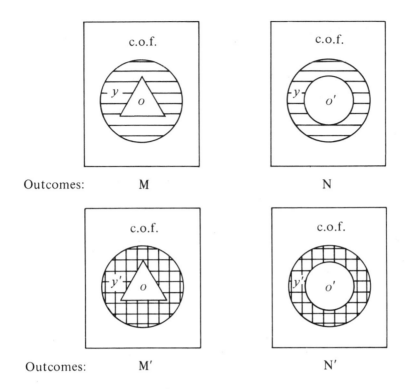

Fig. 2.4. Variation of a parameter in a preference experiment

Outcomes M and N are used to test for preference between o and o' in a c.o.f. that contains y, which is some value of a parametric variable. Outcomes M' and N' are used to test for preference between the same differential outcomes, o and o', in the same c.o.f. with y', a different value of the parameter, substituted for y.

write, "(c.o.f., ω) = c.o.f." This is represented in Fig. 2.3, where Outcome L (c.o.f. alone) is taken to be identical to Outcome O (c.o.f. plus ω).[3]

Such cases are very common in experimental work. So, for example, if a rat turns to the right in a T-maze, it may enter a goalbox that contains food, whereas if it turns left, it enters an identical, but empty, goalbox. Or if a human subject in a decision-making experiment presses one button, he may receive 5¢, whereas if he presses another button, he neither gains nor loses.

It may be easy to set up a comparison between ω and some o as far as events external to the organism are concerned, but it is often harder to do this with respect to the organism's own state. In the examples of the preceding paragraph, it is possible that failure to obtain food or money will arouse in the rat or human being a state of frustration or disappointment that is not present in trials in which the reward is received. If this happens, the nonrewarded trials cannot properly be regarded as having the null differential outcome, ω.

SUMMARY

The three undefined or primitive terms of the present system are *situation, act,* and *outcome.* A situation is made up of all of the circumstances of the environment and of the organism itself that are antecedent to an act. For purposes of comparison, a pair of situations may be analyzed into a *common prior field,* c.p.f., and a pair of *discriminanda, d* and *d'.* The *null discriminandum,* δ, is defined for the special case in which a discriminandum that is present in one situation is lacking in the other.

Whatever an organism may be said to do is an *act.* A special case is an *act of abstention,* α_a, *i.e.,* intentionally not performing some particular act, *a*; this must be distinguished from merely not performing the act.

Outcomes are all of the conditions of the environment and of the organism itself subsequent to an act, including those that are not contingent upon the act. For comparison, two outcomes may be analyzed into a *common outcome field,* c.o.f., and a pair of *differential outcomes, o* and *o'.* The *null differential outcome,* ω, designates the special case in which a differential outcome that is present in one outcome is absent in the other.

NOTES AND COMMENTS

1. It is doubtful that hunger affects taste sensitivity. See, *e.g.,* Pfaffmann and Bare (1950) and Meyer (1952); but, on the other side, Yensen (1959).

2. The statement that latencies, speeds, and amplitudes are properties of acts, but not acts themselves, is not intended to bear one way or another upon Logan's (1956, 1960) "micromolar" theory. But see also the comments on Logan's views in Chapter 11, Note 3, and Chapter 12.

3. Contextual definitions of the null discriminandum, δ, and the null differential outcome, ω, may be offered as follows:

$$(d = \delta) \leftrightarrow [(\text{c.p.f.}, d) = \text{c.p.f.}]. \qquad (2.1)$$
$$(o = \omega) \leftrightarrow [(\text{c.o.f.}, o) = \text{c.o.f.}]. \qquad (2.2)$$

3

Preference and Discrimination

TACTICS OF DEFINITION

In attempting to define a psychological term—for example, *preference* or *discrimination*—, the better part of the task will have been accomplished when the empirical criteria for the factual truth of the assertion, "This organism had such and such a preference (or discrimination) at such and such a time," have been established. Such definition by means of empirical criteria is not "operational" unless the meaning of this term is stretched very far; identification of the meaning of psychological terms with experimental manipulations may once have had corrective value against extreme looseness of conception, but it has also had the effect of sanctifying dull and superficial work and making thought stop short where it is most needed. Rather than beginning with definitions, the following discussion will lead up to them by way of illustration and heuristic argument.

THE DIAGNOSIS OF PREFERENCES

Suppose that a chimpanzee has had experience with two kinds of poker-chip "tokens," white tokens that are exchangeable for grapes in a vending machine and blue tokens for which nothing is given in exchange. Does such experience result in the animal's acquiring a preference for the food tokens over the worthless tokens, and, if so, how are we to discover it? Cowles (1937) performed an experiment that answers both questions.

The experiment is represented in Table 3.1. In outline, it consisted of presenting two situations in an irregular order from trial to trial.[1] In one situation (Conditions 1 and 1') the animal ("Moos") was confronted by two panels side by side, the one on the left bearing a red rectangle on a white ground and the one on the right a green rectangle on a white

Table 3.1

Preference of chimpanzee "Moos" for food tokens
over worthless tokens (Cowles, 1937)

	Conditions			
	Series I		Series II	
	1	2	1'	2'
	d_1 : red left, green right	d_2 : red right, green left	d_1 : red left, green right	d_2 : red right, green left
a_1 : opens left panel	+ o_1 : food token	− o_2 : worthless token	− o_2 : worthless token	+ o_1 : food token
a_2 : opens right panel	− o_2 : worthless token	+ o_1 : food token	+ o_1 : food token	− o_2 : worthless token

Note: d_1 and d_2 are discriminanda; a_1 and a_2 are
alternative acts; o_1 and o_2 are differential outcomes.
The pattern of results is inferred from the fact that a
criterion of 17 successive correct choices was met in
each of the two series. Results were not reported
separately for d_1 and d_2.

ground; the other situation (Conditions 2 and 2') was the same except
that red was on the right and green on the left. The c.p.f. included the
experimental cage, the apparatus, etc.; the discriminanda, d_1 and d_2, were
the displayed pairs of panels, red-left and green-right *vs.* red-right and
green-left. The panels were hinged at the top, and Moos had been trained
to push them inwards to obtain tokens that lay behind them. On any trial,
then, Moos either opened the left panel (Act a_1) or opened the right panel
(Act a_2) and obtained whatever token lay there. Tokens were accu-
mulated and exchanged for food after a group of 36 trials.

Consider Series I in the table. In these trials, Moos obtained a food token by opening the left panel when d_1 was present and by opening the right panel when d_2 was present; he obtained a worthless token if he opened the right panel in the presence of d_1 or the left panel in the presence of d_2. The food tokens and worthless tokens were the differential outcomes, o_1 and o_2, and the c.o.f. included the experimental cage, the apparatus, etc.

The results at the end of training in Series I are indicated by the plus and minus signs in the appropriate cells of the table. These signs represent the fact that Moos predominately opened the left panel when d_1 was present and the right panel when d_2 was present, thus obtaining food tokens more often than worthless tokens. The performance at this stage of learning was in fact almost perfect.

Whether this means that Moos preferred food tokens to worthless tokens cannot, however, be determined without eliminating the possibility that for some reason he simply tended to open the red panel rather than the green one regardless of the outcomes, which would have produced the same results. In other words, the behavior may have been under the control of the discriminanda and unaffected by the differential outcomes. The control for this is obvious, and Cowles carried it out in another series of trials, Series II, observing the same acts in the same situations, but with a reversed relation between act and outcome in each situation. Moos now had to open the right panel with d_1 present and the left panel with d_2 present—and therefore the green panel in each case—to obtain food tokens rather than worthless tokens. That he did so after further training is indicated by the signs in the cells under Series II in the table. The pattern of these signs over all eight cells of the table shows that Moos "tracked" the food tokens throughout the experiment after sufficient experience in each condition, whichever of the two acts was required and whichever position of the panels was present.

Such results will be regarded as evidence sufficient to justify the assertion that Moos expressed a preference for obtaining food tokens over obtaining worthless tokens. Control observations indicated that this preference was acquired as a result of the different exchange values of the tokens and was not an artifact of a preference for white tokens over blue ones.[2]

A second illustration can be drawn from the work of Ellis and Pryer (1958), who were interested in whether a mere one-inch square piece of yellow drawing paper would act as an incentive for feebleminded children in an experiment in which the children were told to try to find the piece of paper when it was hidden beneath one or the other of two objects that

Table 3.2

Preference of mentally defective children for paper square
over null differential outcome, ω (Ellis and Pryer, 1958)

	Conditions			
	Series I		Series II	
	1	2	1'	2'
	d_1: square on left, cylinder on right	d_2: square on right, cylinder on left	d_1: square on left, cylinder on right	d_2: square on right, cylinder on left
a_1: lifts left object	+ o_1: paper square	− o_2: ω	− o_2: ω	+ o_1: paper square
a_2: lifts right object	− o_2: ω	+ o_1: paper square	+ o_1: paper square	− o_2: ω

Note: d_1 and d_2 are discriminanda; a_1 and a_2 are
alternative acts; o_1 and o_2 are differential outcomes.
Series I and II employed different subjects. Results
were not reported separately for d_1 and d_2 or for individual subjects.

constituted discriminanda. The experiment is outlined in Table 3.2. In
Series I the paper was always hidden in a shallow well under a wooden
block two inches square, whereas a wooden cylinder two inches long and
two inches in diameter covered an empty well; the square and cylinder
were arranged to the right and the left of each other randomly over the
trials. In Series II, for which different subjects were used, the conditions
were the same except that the paper was always under the cylinder. The
children were residents of an institution for mental defectives; their mean
age was slightly over 15 years and their mean mental age on the Revised
Stanford-Binet Test was slightly over 5 years. After 50 trials per subject,

the overall percentage of choices of the act that led to obtaining the piece of paper was 70. The pattern of results shown in Table 3.2 is inferred from this, and must have held for at least the 16 subjects who achieved 10 successive correct choices.

If we assume that a particular child who had succeeded in Series I would also have been able to succeed in Series II, which is plausible in the light of many studies of reversal-learning by mental defectives (Stevenson, 1963), the results of Table 3.2 lead to the conclusion that the children, or at least some unknown number of them, demonstrated a preference for the piece of yellow paper over the null differential outcome, ω, when they had been told to try to find the paper. Interestingly enough, Ellis and Pryer found that children matched in mean chronological and mental ages with those of the first experiment performed no better with differential outcomes of a jelly bean and ω than the first group did with the yellow paper and ω. (The effects of instructing the children to find the *empty* well in each experiment were not tested.)

Abstracting from the specific discriminanda, acts, and differential outcomes of the experiments of Cowles and of Ellis and Pryer leaves a table in the form of Tables 3.1 and 3.2 to be filled in with whatever d and d', a and a', and o and o' an experimenter chooses for any particular problem in which he is interested. Such a table will represent what we shall call the *standard preference experiment*. If the results show a pattern like those of Table 3.1, so that under all of the four conditions the subject behaves in such a way as to obtain o more frequently than o', the subject will be said to have exhibited a preference for o over o', given that an appropriate level of statistical significance has been met. The statement, "Outcome o is preferred to Outcome o'," will be written, "oPo'." If significant results in the reverse direction are obtained, so that o' is favored over o in all conditions, the subject will be said to have exhibited a preference for o' over o, and this will be written, "$o'Po$."[3]

INDIFFERENCE

An organism will be said to be *indifferent* between any two differential outcomes, o and o', if it does not prefer o to o' and does not prefer o' to o. This relation will be written, "oIo'," to be read, "The organism is indifferent between Outcomes o and o'," and can be stated formally as follows: by definition, for all o and o',

$$oIo' \leftrightarrow \sim(oPo') \wedge \sim(o'Po). \tag{3.1}$$

To assert indifference is to assert a negative, with the risks that such assertions always entail. So, for example, if Moos had failed to provide evidence that he either preferred food tokens over worthless tokens or preferred worthless tokens over food tokens, one possible conclusion would be that he was indifferent between the two kinds of tokens. On the other hand, a skeptical reader or researcher would have the option of trying to discover some inadequacy in the experiment itself as a test of these preferences, such as insufficient number of training trials, inability of the animal to discriminate between the two panels, emotional upset of the subject resulting from incorrect choices, or what not. To conclude that the subject was indifferent between the outcomes assumes that proper tests were made, a judgment that depends upon the state of knowledge of both method and fact in the field under study.

BIAS

The term "preference," as defined above, is used in a strong sense, to apply only to instances in which choices between acts depend upon differential outcomes of the acts. The word is often used in a weaker sense, when one act of a pair occurs more frequently than another even though this is not due to differential outcomes of the two acts. For such cases we shall use the term "bias."

In discussing Cowles's experiment it was pointed out that the control trials of Series II were needed partly to exclude the possibility that Moos for some unknown reason might have tended to open a red panel rather than a green one, regardless of the differential outcomes of opening the two panels. Had he continued to behave in this way in Series II, he would have shown a bias in both series toward opening the red panel, or away from opening the green panel, and would have failed to show a preference between the two kinds of tokens.

As a further example, consider an experiment by Hess (1956) in which chicks and ducklings with little prior visual experience were given the opportunity to peck at chips of various hues representing the whole spectral range and the nonspectral purples. Hess found that the birds did not peck equally often at chips of different colors but concentrated on some and almost entirely neglected others. For instance, about 24% of all pecks by ducklings were at a green chip (527 nm.) and only about 1% were at an orange chip (601 nm.). Hess offered the results as representing "natural preferences" for objects of different colors. No differential outcomes of pecking at the various chips were provided, however, and unless the behavior was affected by subtle and unknown differences in the

Table 3.3

Color bias in ducklings

(hypothetical—inferred from results of Hess, 1956)

	Conditions	
	1	2
	d_1: green on left, orange on right	d_2: orange on left, green on right
a_1: pecks at color on left	+ o_1: ?	− o_2: ?
a_2: pecks at color on right	− o_2: ?	+ o_1: ?

Note: d_1 and d_2 are discriminanda; a_1 and a_2 are alternative acts. No differential outcomes, o_1 and o_2, were provided.

consequences of pecking at one color rather than another, the chicks and ducklings were exhibiting only what we would call biases, not preferences.

Hess's experiment did not involve binary choices and trial-by-trial analysis; rather, the subjects were exposed to many colors simultaneously and pecked freely among them. Suppose, however, we imagine an experiment in which on any trial the subject is confronted by two chips, a green one and an orange one, with the relative position of the chips changed randomly from trial to trial. Table 3.3 outlines the experiment. Hess's experiment suggests that the results would be as indicated in the table, that is, that the birds would tend to peck more often at the green than at the orange. The relative frequency of pecks to the left would then be greater in Condition 1, with green on the left, than in Condition 2, with green on the right. (Observe the resemblance to Series I of Tables 3.1 and 3.2.) If we have been careful not to provide differential outcomes of the two acts and if there are none that have escaped our attention, then there are no outcomes to reverse and no preference (in the strong sense) would or could be identified from these data. This is no criticism of Hess's experiment; what is at issue is the use of the word "preference" and, more importantly, a distinction between two concepts, that of preference in the strong sense and that of bias.

When the author of an elaborate mathematical analysis of the shapes assumed by soap-bubbles packed closely together finds that bubbles assume one of two possible shapes more often than the other and speaks of the bubbles' "preferring" the more frequent shape, one can make allowance for his lightening a dry argument by mathematicians' whimsy. But if a psychologist finds that a rat tends on its initial trials in a maze to turn right more often than left, and calls this a "position preference," we may not know whether he intends the word "preference" in the strong sense or a weaker one. If he intends the weaker meaning, "position bias" would be a less ambiguous phrase. The fact that infants look oftener or longer at some colors or visual figures than others is insufficient evidence for color or shape preferences, as this term is used here. The same may be said for "ear preferences" that are defined solely by the fact that subjects who have one-syllable nouns presented simultaneously, one to one ear and one to the other, tend to recall those that are presented to a particular ear better than those presented to the other.

The experimental literature is replete with cases like these; often there is little doubt that nothing stronger than a bias was intended by the writer, but sometimes genuine doubt arises and one would like to know what was meant and the grounds for it. The reader has to ask himself whether the acts had differential outcomes and, if so, whether there is reason to suppose that the relative frequencies of the acts were associated with them. If not, no more than a bias was proved.

It is important for the student to note that an organism may perfectly well have a preference even if a particular experiment fails to show it. Thus, for example, we cannot conclude from Table 3.3 that the subjects had no preferences among the patches of colors. The hypothetical experiment was not designed for the diagnosis of preferences, since differential outcomes were not provided; remember, also, the remarks about asserting a negative, in the section on Indifference, above.

Behavioral biases are of various types and are frequently interesting in their own right. A vigorous kick of the leg is more likely than a weak one if the patellar tendon is struck sharply; a similar rough rule holds for eyelid closure to a loud sound; and other such cases are easy to think of. In such "reflexes," there is no reason to imagine the existence of a preference, in spite of the strong biases. In highly automatized features of acts, such as speaking with a regional or foreign accent, the person does indeed make certain speech-sounds rather than others, and may have learned to do so because of differential outcomes of speaking in particular ways in his childhood. This sensitivity to differential outcomes may persist into adulthood. The writer has heard a friend say of a mutual acquaintance that she retains her Russian accent because she thinks it sounds attractive, and this analysis may be correct. When, however, an accent remains despite its leading to aversive consequences, it is classifiable as an automatized characteristic of habitual behavior, and hence as an instance of bias but not of preference.[4] In general, clearcut cases of reflexes, tropisms, orienting behavior (taxes), and instinctive acts are good candidates for the study of biases unassociated with preferences, especially in very young and inexperienced organisms; it is nevertheless dangerous to decide the issue merely on the basis of the presumed behavior-class membership of an act.[5]

Nothing prevents the same set of data from showing both a preference and a bias that is unrelated to it. Suppose, for example, that Moos, the chimpanzee of Cowles's experiment, had a bias toward opening the left panel. This would be shown in Table 3.1 by a reliably greater total number of instances of a_1 than of a_2 over all conditions taken together. If the bias were strong enough—that is, if the entries in the first row of cells amounted to nearly 100% and those in the second row to nearly 0%, the preference would not show through and other acts or discriminanda would need to be tried; but there is enough freedom for a weaker bias than this to exhibit itself without obscuring the preference. Note that this tendency to open the lefthand panel, like a right-turning bias in a maze, would be what is commonly called a "response bias." It would be associated with the c.p.f. or some feature of it but, unlike the behavior of Hess's chicks and ducklings, would not necessarily vary with the discriminanda.

PREFERENCE, DIFFERENTIAL OUTCOMES, AND THE COMMON OUTCOME FIELD

Our conclusion from the discussion of Cowles's experiment was that Moos had exhibited a preference for the differential outcome of obtaining food tokens over that of obtaining worthless tokens. Likewise, Ellis and Pryer's children were said to have preferred a paper square to the null differential outcome, ω. Representing the preference relation by P and the differential outcomes by o and o', we write "oPo'." It must now be pointed out that this constitutes an abstraction from the actual state of affairs. The outcomes of the acts always involved the c.o.f. as well as one of the differential outcomes; it would therefore be closer to the facts to indicate this by writing "(c.o.f., o)P(c.o.f., o')." Referring back to Fig. 2.3, the experiments showed preferences for Outcome M over Outcome N (Cowles) and Outcome M over Outcome O (Ellis and Pryer), rather than merely for o over o' in the former case and o over ω in the latter.

The practice of treating preference as a relation between differential outcomes and of omitting reference to the c.o.f. is universal and economical. Nevertheless, it can lead to theoretical confusion if it makes us forget the c.o.f. when we come to interpret preferences and attempt to discover their laws. The question is, to what extent is a preference for o over o' independent of the c.o.f. in which this preference is found? If preferences were altogether at the mercy of c.o.f.'s, the usefulness of preference as a scientific concept would be in doubt and perhaps it never would have been invented. On the other hand, it is obvious that complete independence does not obtain, and that it is an experimental question how variation in the c.o.f. would affect the preference relation between an o and o'. This has already been indicated by the discussion of parameters in Chapter 2.

THE DIAGNOSIS OF DISCRIMINATIONS

That there is a close relation between tests of preference and tests of discrimination is shown by the fact that positive results in a standard preference experiment cannot be obtained unless the subject discriminates between whatever discriminanda are offered in the experiment. Because discrimination is less central than preference in what follows, and because there are parallels between the two concepts, discrimination will require less discussion than preference. Before considering the relation between the two concepts more closely, let us look at illustrative experiments the purpose of which was to investigate discrimination.

Marsh (1964) studied discrimination in nursery-school children 36 to 48 months of age under several conditions, and Table 3.4 represents one of his experiments. The child was confronted on each trial by two plastic tumblers of the same shape and size, one black and the other white, with the left-right positions of the two tumblers randomized over trials. The child was to find a marble that was hidden under one of the tumblers; the marble was always under the black tumbler in Series I and always under the white tumbler in Series II, and the child was permitted to lift only one tumbler on each trial. Trials proceeded with each subject until a criterion of eight successive correct trials out of 10 was achieved in the first series,

Table 3.4
Discrimination between black and white tumblers
by a nursery school child (Marsh, 1964)

	Conditions			
	Series I		Series II	
	1	2	1′	2′
	d_1: black on left, white on right	d_2: white on left, black on right	d_1: black on left, white on right	d_2: white on left, black on right
a_1: lifts left tumbler	+ o_1: marble	− o_2: ω	− o_2: ω	+ o_1: marble
a_2: lifts right tumbler	− o_2: ω	+ o_1: marble	+ o_1: marble	− o_2: ω

Note: d_1 and d_2 are discriminanda; a_1 and a_2 are
alternative acts; o_1 and o_2 are differential outcomes.

at which point the second series was run to the same criterion without further instructions.

All of the subjects met the criteria in both Series I and Series II, although of course some required more trials than others. Data were not reported for the separate conditions of Table 3.4, but the criterion was such that during the last 10 trials in each series a child must have given results such as those represented in the table. Putting aside questions of the statistical reliability of the results for individual children as unlikely to be critical for the point, it can be concluded that the children displayed discrimination between the two tumblers.

As might be expected, the discrimination was easy for the children. (Marsh's interest lay in comparing their behavior under the conditions described here with that under other conditions that are irrelevant to our present purpose.) But with respect to the illustration, note that if a child were tested in only one series, we would not know whether he was showing a discrimination between the two tumblers or merely a differential response to them. Results like those of Series I would be produced by a child who was quite unaffected by the differential outcomes of his acts and was merely lifting the black tumbler on every trial; this is what would happen, for example, if children had "instinctive" tendencies, in the ethological sense, to handle the darker of two objects. But if such were the case, it should be difficult or impossible for the child to succeed under the reversal conditions of Series II, and children who started with Series II should give results like those of children who started with Series I. The latter point is often relied upon by experimenters who use different subjects in the two series, as in the next illustration.

Table 3.5 outlines part of an experiment by Lashley (1938) on rats' ability to discriminate between circles of different diameters. The apparatus was a jumping stand devised by Lashley in which the animals were trained to jump a gap from a small platform through one or the other of two small windows onto a goal platform. In a test situation, a card with a figure on it stood in each door; if the rat jumped to the correct window, it knocked down the card, landed on the goal platform, and received food, but if it jumped to the incorrect window, the card was locked and the animal bumped its nose and fell into a net below. There was a circle 9 cm. in diameter on one card and one of 12 cm. on the other; their left-right positions were randomized over the trials. The discriminanda, then, were the pairs of cards (or of circles); d_1 was the case with the smaller circle on the left and the larger on the right, and d_2 was the case with the two cards reversed. On any trial the animal jumped to the left (a_1) or jumped to the right (a_2). The differential outcomes were landing on the goal platform and receiving food (o_1) vs. bumping the nose on a locked card and falling into the net (o_2). In Series I, food was obtained by jumping left when the smaller circle was on the left and by jumping right when the smaller circle was on the right (thus, by jumping to the smaller circle in each case); in Series II, the relation was reversed, and the rat obtained food by jumping to the side with the larger circle.

Lashley's rats solved this problem and reached a criterion of 20 successive errorless trials in each series. No reversal of the relation between acts and outcomes was performed with individual animals, but rather some subjects were run in Series I and others in Series II, a procedure that was commented upon above. The known capacities of rats to do reversal learning would lead us, however, to suppose that individual animals would behave in accordance with the group results described in Table 3.5 as a whole and thereby show that their behavior was sensitive to its differential outcomes. On this supposition, we conclude that the subjects exhibited

Table 3.5
Discrimination between circles of different
diameters by rats (Lashley, 1938)

	Conditions			
	Series I		Series II	
	1	2	1'	2'
	d_1 : circles: 9 cm. on left, 12 cm. on right	d_2 : circles: 12 cm. on left, 9 cm. on right	d_1 : circles: 9 cm. on left, 12 cm. on right	d_2 : circles: 12 cm. on left, 9 cm. on right
a_1 : jumps left	+ o_1 : food	− o_2 : bumps door, falls into net	− o_2 : bumps door, falls into net	+ o_1 : food
a_2 : jumps right	− o_2 : bumps door, falls into net	+ o_1 : food	+ o_1 : food	− o_2 : bumps door, falls into net

Note: d_1 and d_2 are discriminanda; a_1 and a_2 are
alternative acts; o_1 and o_2 are differential outcomes.
Series I and II were run on different subjects.

discrimination between the two arrangements of the pair of cards and
therefore, presumably, between the circles of different diameter.[6] (But
see Note 8.)

If one abstracts from the specific discriminanda, acts, and differential
outcomes of Marsh's and Lashley's experiments and leaves tables like
Tables 3.4 and 3.5 to be filled in with whatever d and d', a and a', and o
and o' the experimenter chooses for whatever problem interests him, the

table will represent what will be called the *standard discrimination experiment*. The subject will be said to have displayed a discrimination between d and d' if the experiment gives a pattern of results like those of Tables 3.4 and 3.5 at an acceptable level of significance.

The statement, "Discriminandum d is discriminated from Discriminandum d'," will be written, "dDd'." If an organism discriminates between d and δ, *i.e.*, if $dD\delta$, it will be said to have *detected d*.

DIFFERENTIAL RESPONSE

Like "preference," the term "discrimination" is ambiguous in common usage. In its strong sense, as defined by the standard discrimination experiment, it refers to instances in which choices depend upon differential outcomes of the acts. But it is frequently used in a weaker sense, to refer merely to the fact that the relative frequencies of two acts are different in one situation than in another. The term *differential response* will be used here for this weaker sense. In contrast to "bias," "differential response" does not refer to the direction of the effect.

In discussing bias, it was mentioned that the vigor of a leg-kick to a blow on the patellar tendon ("patellar tendon reflex" or "knee-jerk") depends upon the strength of the blow, which anyone can readily demonstrate for himself. Imagine, however, an experiment of the form of Table 3.6, in which weak and strong blows, the forces of which are measured by some appropriate instrument, are administered in random order and at random times to a human subject, and in which the extent of the kick in response to each blow is also measured. It can be seen that results like those of the table could be obtained if proper forces of blow and an appropriate setting of the distinction between large and small kicks were chosen. These results would satisfy the definition of differential response, since the relative frequencies of the two acts varied with the discriminanda. No second series, with reversal of differential outcomes, could be carried out, since no such outcomes were provided. Unless we suppose that such differential outcomes existed undetected and that the results would be reversed if these differential outcomes were reversed as in a discrimination experiment, the fact that the behavior following d_1 is different from that following d_2 does not constitute evidence that a discrimination, in the strong sense, has been made between these discriminanda. (The student is warned once more about negative assertions. The subject may have discriminated the hammer blows, but the experiment as described could not show this.)

Table 3.6
Differential response of human patellar reflex
(hypothetical experiment)

	Conditions	
	1	2
	d_1: weak blow	d_2: strong blow
a_1: small kick	+ o_1 : ?	− o_2 : ?
a_2: large kick	− o_2 : ?	+ o_1 : ?

Note: d_1 and d_2 are discriminanda; a_1 and a_2 are alternative acts. No differential outcomes, o_1 and o_2, were provided.

DISCRIMINATION, DISCRIMINANDA, AND THE COMMON PRIOR FIELD

Just as preference is universally taken to be a relation between differential outcomes, abstracted from the c.o.f., so discrimination is taken to be a relation between discriminanda, abstracted from the c.p.f. Thus, discrimination between Situations B and C, or B and D, of Fig. 2.1 would be treated as discrimination between d and d' or between d and δ. The same kinds of problems arise in the two cases. When we say that Lashley's rats discriminated between circles of different diameters, we omit reference to the rest of the situation in which they were tested—the apparatus, the laboratory room with its various sights, sounds, and smells, the state of the animals themselves, and the like. Thus, instead of writing, "(c.p.f., d)D(c.p.f., d')," to indicate that the rats discriminated between two whole situations, one of which contained d and the other, d', we write simply, "dDd'." In any particular test situation, no doubt there are features that are quite irrelevant to the behavior, but, as suggested in Chapter 2, it is always possible, or even probable, that there are other features that affect the discrimination, or its keenness. It is perhaps more common for research on discrimination to concern itself with these latter features as parameters than for research on preference to do this, although neglect of such parametric variables is risky in either case.

RELATIONS BETWEEN PREFERENCE AND DISCRIMINATION

The reader has undoubtedly observed that the standard discrimination experiment is identical in form to the standard preference experiment. Even the details of Ellis and Pryer's preference experiment (Table 3.2) with children and Marsh's discrimination experiment (Table 3.4), also with children, are very similar. Whether the object is to determine whether a particular preference exists or to determine whether a particular discrimination exists, the evidence will come from observation of acts under the very same manipulation of discriminanda and differential outcomes. The experiment may be called a *standard discrimination-preference experiment* when there is no need to distinguish the purpose for which it was carried out. Its abstract form is shown in Table 3.7.

It follows that an organism cannot exhibit a preference in such a standard experiment without also exhibiting a discrimination and, conversely, that it cannot exhibit a discrimination in such an experiment without also exhibiting a preference. In Cowles's experiment, if Moos had been confronted with a pair of discriminanda that he could not discriminate between, his problem of obtaining food tokens rather than worthless tokens would have been insoluble; hence, although he preferred the former to the latter, as Table 3.1 shows, he could not have shown this fact under those circumstances. Similarly, if Lashley's rats had been indifferent between the outcome of getting food and that of bumping the nose and falling into the net, the fact that they were able to discriminate between circles 9 and 12 cm. in diameter, as demonstrated in Table 3.5, would not have come to light. Or, putting it differently, Cowles's experiment, whatever his purpose, is precisely as good a demonstration of Moos's discrimination between the two pairs of panels as it is of his preference for food tokens over worthless tokens, and Lashley's experiment is precisely as good a demonstration that his rats preferred getting food to bumping their noses and falling into the net as it is that they discriminated between the two pairs of circles.

The practical difference between a standard experiment on preference and one on discrimination is that when one wants to diagnose a preference, one tries to make sure from previous knowledge that the required discrimination is easy, and when one wants to diagnose a discrimination, one provides differential outcomes one of which is believed, from

Table 3.7
Form of the standard discrimination-preference experiment

	Conditions			
	Series I		Series II	
	1	2	1'	2'
	d	d'	d	d'
a	+ o	− o'	− o'	+ o
a'	− o'	+ o	+ o	− o'

Note: d and d' are discriminanda; a and a' are alternative acts; o and o' are differential outcomes. Results such as are represented by the plus and minus signs would indicate that dDd' and oPo'; if the plus and minus signs were interchanged in each column, they would indicate that dDd' and $o'Po$.

previous experience, to be definitely preferred to the other. If the results are positive, the selection of discriminanda or differential outcomes, as the case may be, is shown to have been adequate; but if they are negative, one must consider the question whether the selection was adequate before concluding that the preference or discrimination being tested for does not exist.

The coincidence of the standard experiment-forms for preference and discrimination, and the resulting fact that the same data supply information about both states, will not occasion too much surprise if it is kept in mind that different aspects of the data are employed for the two purposes. In the case of preference, we look at the choices as they are related to the outcomes of the acts; in the case of discrimination, we consider the choices as they are related to the discriminanda that are present at the time the acts are chosen between. Furthermore, as will be seen in Chapter 4, preference is an asymmetric relation between the differential outcomes, whereas discrimination is a symmetric relation between the discriminanda. This enables an organism to exhibit a preference in either direction between the differential outcomes while still exhibiting the same discrimination between the discriminanda. For example, in Cowles's experiment, if Moos were tested when for some reason he preferred worthless tokens to food tokens, this would be shown in Table 3.1 by the plus and minus signs being interchanged in each column. The data would then show the new preference, but would continue to show the discrimination between the pairs of colored panels, as before.[7]

From the point of view of an SAO system, preference and discrimination are fundamental psychological concepts. Beyond this, however, the fact that both states are diagnosed by means of a single standard form of experiment means that the two concepts stand on the same footing and are *equally* fundamental.

SUMMARY

In accordance with the principle that definitions of psychological concepts rest upon prescription of their empirical criteria, a standard form of experiment for the diagnosis of *preference* was presented. In this experiment, an organism chooses between two alternative acts in the presence of one or the other of two discriminanda; if the predominant choice is such as to obtain one rather than the other of two differential outcomes in all combinations of discriminanda and acts, the former outcome is said to be preferred to the latter.

An organism is said to be *indifferent* between two outcomes if it prefers neither outcome to the other.

The standard experimental form for diagnosis of *discrimination* is identical to that for preference. Hence, if a preference is exhibited in such an experiment, so also is a discrimination, and if a discrimination is exhibited, so also is a preference. Preference, however, is an asymmetric relation between a pair of differential outcomes, whereas discrimination is a symmetric relation between a pair of discriminanda. The two concepts are fundamental in an SAO system, and equally so.

If an organism performs one of a pair of alternative acts more frequently than the other under constant conditions, the organism is said to exhibit a *bias* toward the more frequent act. If the relative frequencies of two acts are different in the presence of one discriminandum than in the presence of another, the organism is said to exhibit *differential response* to the discriminanda. The terms *bias* and *differential response* do not imply that the behavior is sensitive to its outcomes; hence they are weaker than *preference* and *discrimination*, which do imply this.

NOTES AND COMMENTS

1. The requirement that conditions involving d and d' be presented in an irregular or, better, a random order in preference and discrimination experiments is imposed in order to prevent the subject from using the act and its outcome on one trial as a predictor of the outcome of an act on another trial without recourse to the discriminanda.

2. In reducing the description of an experiment like that of Cowles to the form of Table 3.1, much detail is necessarily neglected. In particular, it should be mentioned that Cowles used a "correction" procedure; that is, on trials in which Moos opened the "wrong" panel and obtained a worthless token, he was permitted to open the other panel and obtain a food token. Thus, Outcome o_1 was obtaining a food token, and Outcome o_2 was obtaining a worthless token, opening the other panel, and obtaining a food token, a more complex outcome than Table 3.1 indicates. One might argue that the experiment demonstrates a preference for getting a food token directly rather than by a longer route; but it still seems reasonable to conclude that Moos was showing a preference for food tokens over worthless tokens.

3. It would be possible to add a subscript or superscript to identify the organism in such a formula as "oPo'," but this complication does not appear to be necessary. The same can be said about identifying the time (*i.e.*, the exact date) for which the assertion is made.

4. Labov (1963) has presented striking evidence of widespread alterations in certain speech sounds of members of a group toward conformity with the speech of a prestigious "reference group." Individuals' speech seemed to become symptomatic of their strength of "identification" with the reference group.

5. It is riskier than it once seemed to be to assume that reflexes, especially those under control of the autonomic nervous system, are insensitive to their outcomes. This question will be discussed further in Chapter 12, Note 3.

6. Lashley's work, from which Table 3.5 was drawn, was intended not merely to show that rats could discriminate between circles of different diameters but to determine the limits of such discrimination. Lashley found that the discrimination held until the ratio of the two diameters being compared fell below 1.3 to 1.

7. Although discrimination is defined as a relation between discriminanda and preference as a relation between outcomes, it is obviously possible for a pair of objects that constitute the d and d' in a discrimination experiment to be employed as the o and o' in another experiment. A subject can be tested for his ability to discriminate between the tones of a clarinet and an oboe, using the tones as d and d', and he can also be tested for his preference for hearing one of these tones rather than the other, using them as o and o'. In the former experiment one would use something other than the tones as differential outcomes; in the latter experiment, one would use something other than the tones as the discriminanda. It is true that Wilson (1959) performed an experiment in which he used the numbers of food pellets visible to a monkey through the lid of a box as discriminanda, and the numbers of pellets contained in the box when it was open (the discriminanda disappearing in the process of opening the box) as differential outcomes; but, although this is amusing, it can hardly be recommended as a standard procedure.

8. What we have called the "standard discrimination-preference experiment" commonly goes by the name "discrimination-reversal experiment." The examples from Marsh and Lashley are both instances of "simultaneous discrimination"; that is, the two tumblers (Marsh) and the two circles (Lashley) were always presented simultaneously, and their spatial position was varied from trial to trial. In such cases, as the text notes, d was always a pair of tumblers or circles and d' was always the same pair with reversed right-left positions. Strictly speaking, it is these *pairs* that are discriminated between; it is a separate step to conclude that, since the pairs were discriminated and since they could not have been discriminated had the tumblers or circles not differed, the tumblers and circles themselves were discriminated. In a "successive discrimination" procedure, only one of the tumblers or circles would be presented on any trial, and the tumblers or circles would be presented in random order from trial to trial. A direct inference that the tumblers or circles were discriminated would then be possible. Examples of successive discrimination are experiments by Besch, Morris, and Levine (Table 9.1) and Jenkins and Hanratty (Table 9.2).

But in fact the problem is even more subtle than this, as the history of studies of simultaneous discrimination learning since Spence's paper of 1936 testifies. It is possible to imagine, for example, that Lashley's rats were not comparing the two configurations of the small and large circles but were jumping, say, toward or away from the small circle and not "attending" to the large circle. Although in the present experiment this would amount to discrimination between the two configurations, in the extreme it would make the discrimination psychologically equivalent to detection of the position of the small circle; and the acts that are classified in Table 3.5 as jumping to the left and jumping to the right could therefore be interpreted and reclassified as jumping to and jumping away from the small circle, according to the position of this circle. Other possibilities exist, as can be seen in the review by Lovejoy (1968). That the question is not trivial is shown in the same review by the large effort that has gone into the development of theories that answer it in different ways and of experimental work devoted to testing these theories.

In the writer's opinion, the successive discrimination procedure is fundamental and the simultaneous discrimination procedure, however useful, is secondary. Not only does a conclusion about discrimination require at least one less logical step in the former case than in the latter, as pointed out above, but it is hard to see how certain elementary questions can be answered at all except by the successive method—for example, Jenkins and Hanratty's question whether an organism can discriminate between two intensities of one of its own states (see Chapter 9). Indeed, work with simultaneous discrimination appears to have dealt more with problems of theory of learning and attention than with matters specifically concerned with discrimination itself.

4

Desire, Aversion,
and the Affective Scale

If an organism is tested for its preferences among a number of differential outcomes, some sort of order may be expected to appear among these outcomes. Two assumptions are commonly made about this order: (1) that the objects will arrange themselves along what may be called an *affective scale*, with differences in preference value represented by the distances between objects on the scale or at least by the rank order of the objects, and (2) that the affective scale is divided by a neutral point into two segments, one containing objects that are pleasant, rewarding, or desirable, and the other containing objects that are unpleasant, punishing, or aversive. Both of these assumptions require discussion.

LOGICAL PROPERTIES OF PREFERENCE

Because it always connects two objects, preference (*P*) is called a *binary relation*. We shall suppose that this relation is *irreflexive, asymmetric,* and *transitive at a given moment of time, with the c.p.f. and the c.o.f. held constant.*

To say that preference is irreflexive is to say that an organism cannot prefer an outcome to itself; *e.g.,* Moos cannot be shown to prefer food tokens to identical food tokens. In symbols: for all o,

$$\sim(oPo). \tag{4.1}$$

To say that preference is asymmetric is to say that if o is preferred to o', then o' is not preferred to o. Asymmetry gives preference a directional quality; thus, if Moos is shown to prefer food tokens to worthless tokens, he is thereby shown not to prefer worthless tokens to food tokens. In symbols: for all o and o',

$$oPo' \rightarrow \sim(o'Po). \tag{4.2}$$

To say that preference is transitive is to say that if an organism prefers one outcome to a second and the second to a third, then it prefers the first to the third. Thus, if Moos prefers a food token to a worthless token and also prefers a worthless token to ω, we may conclude without further information that he prefers a food token to ω. In symbols: for all o, o', and o'',

$$oPo' \wedge o'Po'' \rightarrow oPo''. \tag{4.3}$$

It is important to remember that (4.1), (4.2), *and* (4.3) *are asserted only under the conditions stated above.* The preference value of differential outcomes may vary from time to time or with variation in the c.p.f. or the c.o.f. One might be fond of a person at one time and hate him at another; if irreflexivity (and transitivity) are unrestricted with respect to time, this would violate (4.1) because it would mean that in comparison with some constant outcome, the person (at one time) is preferred to himself (at another time). Similarly, if someone prefers roast beef to pie at the beginning of a meal, and prefers pie to ice cream at the end of the meal, disregard of time and changes in the c.p.f. and c.o.f. would lead by (4.3) to the conclusion that the subject prefers roast beef to ice cream; but this might be true at one time, such as the beginning of the meal, and not at another, such as the end of the meal.

The assumptions that preference is irreflexive and asymmetric, under the stated restrictions, are implicit in the empirical criteria of preference that were presented in Chapter 3. It is obvious that no standard preference experiment could show that a differential outcome was preferred to itself or that both oPo' and $o'Po$ held in the same data. The case is different, however, with respect to transitivity; the empirical criteria have nothing to say about this. The assumption that preference is transitive, given the stated restrictions, goes beyond these criteria; furthermore, it is not capable of direct experimental test, which would require that three preferences be determined simultaneously. Nevertheless, it is a useful assumption for several reasons. First, it puts order into what otherwise would be an unsystematized set of outcomes and permits us to develop an affective scale. Second, it suggests that if there are intransitivities in a set of preferences, then the c.p.f. or the c.o.f. was not under adequate control. Finally, it leads to the expectation that the closer an experiment approaches to the ideal of simultaneous tests, the less evidence of intransitivity there should be. Of course, if in the long run the systematic gain from the assumption should come to be less than the burden of assuming it, it would have to be given up; but this would have serious consequences.[1]

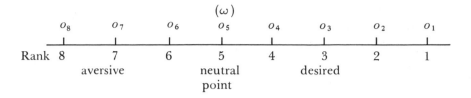

Fig. 4.1. An affective scale

Of the eight outcomes, o_1 is the most preferred and o_8 the most dispreferred. Each outcome is preferred to all of the outcomes to its left. Outcomes o_1-o_4 are desired; Outcomes o_6-o_8 are aversive.

THE AFFECTIVE SCALE

If the preference relation over a set of objects is irreflexive, asymmetric, and transitive, then these objects can be arranged in order along an affective scale, as indicated in Fig. 4.1. Consider points on the line in the figure. In the case of any pair of these points, one can be said to be to the right of the other. But the relation of *being to the right of* is irreflexive, asymmetric, and transitive, as the reader can convince himself by a little reflection; and since these are also properties of preference, we can take points on the line to represent the positions of various objects of preference as long as any object that is preferred to another object is represented as being to the right of that other object. So, in the figure, Outcome o_1 is to the right of all other outcomes, and is thus represented as being preferred to all of them. Outcome o_3 is to the right of, and preferred to, Outcome o_4 and all other outcomes to its left; and so on. At present we are not concerned with distances between pairs of outcomes; only the relative positions count. It can be seen that this scale constitutes a *rank order*, with o_1 in first place as most preferred, o_2 in second place, o_3 in third place, etc. Observe, in particular, that we could not arrange the outcomes in a rank order without transitivity. For example, according to the scale, o_5 is preferred to o_6 and o_6 is preferred to o_7; if, now, o_5 were *not* preferred to o_7, how could these three outcomes be placed properly along the line?

Desire and Aversion

As was pointed out in the beginning of this chapter, psychologists have usually believed, not only that an affective scale exists, but also that it has a neutral point that divides it into a "positive" or desired segment and a "negative" or aversive segment. If we look for some outcome that might serve to identify the neutral point, the unique status of the null differential outcome, ω, comes to mind. This particular differential outcome has some of the properties of the number zero, which divides numbers into positive and negative series (*cf.* the definition of ω in Note 3, Chapter 2). Furthermore, one way of asking oneself whether some outcome of low preference value is desired or aversive is to ask, "Would I prefer it to happen rather than not?", an affirmative answer to which would mean that the outcome had at least some "positive" value; whereas if the answer were, "I would prefer its not happening to its happening," the outcome would appear to be "negative" or aversive. But this can be expressed precisely in terms of preferences with respect to ω, as in the following definitions.

> By definition, for all o, an organism *desires* an outcome, o, and o is a *desired outcome*, if and only if $oP\omega$.   (4.4)

> By definition, for all o, an organism *is aversive to* an outcome, o, and o is an *aversive outcome*, if and only if ωPo.   (4.5)

With these definitions it is clear that Outcomes o_1 through o_4 in Fig. 4.1 are all desired, since they are all preferred to ω, and that Outcomes o_6 through o_8 are all aversive, since ω is preferred to all of them.

When ω is used to divide the affective scale into desired and aversive segments in this way, it will be said to locate the *affective zero* of the scale.

From these definitions and the transitivity of preference it follows at once that if an organism desires an outcome, o, and is aversive to an outcome, o', then it prefers o to o', whatever these outcomes may be. If I desire to see Person A and am aversive to seeing Person B, then I prefer seeing A to seeing B. That is, for all o and o',

> if o is desired and o' is aversive, then oPo'.   (4.6)

Two useful principles that permit desires and aversions to be established indirectly can likewise be derived from the definitions and the transitivity of P. First, for all o and o',

> if oPo' and o' is desired, then o is desired.   (4.7)

For example, Spragg (1940) found that a chimpanzee that had had periodic injections of morphine preferred obtaining the syringe and an injection of morphine to obtaining a banana, under conditions in which it desired the banana. Accordingly, as is justified by (4.7), he concluded that the animal desired the syringe and injection.

Second, for all o and o',

$$\text{if } o \text{ is aversive and } oPo', \text{ then } o' \text{ is aversive.} \tag{4.8}$$

For example, if Rodgers and Rozin's (1966) thiamine-deprived rats were aversive to eating the deficient diet upon which they had been fed, and yet preferred eating this deficient diet to being in a state of hunger, then being hungry was even more aversive than eating the diet. (This was not necessarily these authors' opinion, and they did not directly test the aversiveness of being hungry.) If the deep sea is preferred to the devil and is itself aversive, then the devil is, as he should be, even more aversive than the deep sea.

Principles (4.7) and (4.8) are convenient whenever one wishes to know whether some outcome is desired or aversive and already knows the status of an outcome that can be compared with the first for its preference value, and also for cases in which the desiredness or aversiveness of an outcome needs to be determined, but the outcome happens to be difficult to compare directly with ω.

LOGICAL PROPERTIES OF INDIFFERENCE

The outcomes in Fig. 4.1 were chosen so that each of them was preferred to the one adjacent to it on the left and, therefore, to all outcomes to its left. No instances of indifference between two outcomes were included, and these must now be considered. Because indifference was defined in Chapter 3 as a relation between two outcomes such that neither is preferred to the other, it may seem natural to the reader that outcomes between which an organism is indifferent should be regarded as "tied" in the rank order and belonging at the same point on the affective scale. Although this view has often been taken, the problem is more difficult and interesting than first appears.

Consider what logical properties the binary relation of indifference (I) should have. By the nature of the empirical criteria of indifference, it must be reflexive; for example, Moos must be indifferent between a food token and an identical food token. In symbols: for all o,

$$oIo. \tag{4.9}$$

By the same empirical criteria, indifference must be symmetric; if Moos is indifferent between a food token and a worthless token, he is also indifferent between a worthless token and a food token. In symbols: for all o and o',

$$oIo' \rightarrow o'Io. \qquad (4.10)$$

The matter of transitivity, however, cannot be resolved so readily. Suppose that we test a child for his preferences among three soft drinks, a, b, and c, and find that he has no preference either way between a and b and between b and c, so that we can write for him aIb and bIc. If indifference is transitive, then we can conclude from this without further testing that he has no preference either way between a and c, that is, that aIc. If, nevertheless, we run the test, is it certain to show indifference between a and c? Obviously, the answer is no; the results of an experimental procedure are never certain in advance. In this case, however, the uncertainty does not rest merely upon the fact that the tests are not simultaneous and that the subject's state may change between tests.

The problem may be clarified by noticing that it arises in tests of discrimination, as well as of preference. Imagine that a subject is tested for color discrimination among three very similar colors, x, y, and z. Then he may fail to discriminate between x and y and between y and z and nevertheless discriminate between x and z. Thus, like indifference, failure to discriminate may not be transitive. This could happen in the following way. Suppose that x is some wavelength of light, that y is a slightly longer wavelength, and that z is a still longer wavelength. Then, since no subject can discriminate perfectly and no method of testing is without error, the results may fail to show discrimination between x and y and between y and z and yet show discrimination of the somewhat larger difference between x and z. Such a phenomenon is not peculiar to the behavior of living beings; it is entirely possible to have a pan balance that responds differentially to two weights of, say, 50.1 and 50.3 gm., although it fails to differentiate between 50.1 and 50.2 and between 50.2 and 50.3. Returning now to the problem of preference, soft drinks a and c might differ sufficiently in whatever properties determine affective value to produce a detectable preference for one of them over the other, although this was not so for a versus b or b versus c. In that case indifference would fail to be transitive.

It was pointed out in Chapter 3 that a failure to discover a preference between two outcomes can sometimes be interpreted, not as an indication of indifference, but as resulting from a failure to use an adequate method. Such a conclusion would be obvious, for example, if the experiment employed discriminanda between which the subject was unable to discriminate. Aside from this, different experiments may use methods that differ in sensitivity for any of a large number of reasons, including differences in degree of control of extraneous sources of error. Furthermore, to assert that a preference is shown by a set of data requires the choice of some statistical criterion for the significance of the contingencies in the data; if the criterion is not met by the observations, it might be met if twice as many observations were made. Hence, it is always possible that one experimenter may detect a preference where another failed to do so. The critic must judge as best he can whether the conditions were satisfactory in any case in which indifference is claimed. On the other hand, infinite sensitivity and perfect control of conditions are unrealizable ideals. If no preference is found, but a critic believes that one would be found with a better method, the question still remains whether, even if found, it would be strong enough to make a difference; if not, the argument would be idle.

Neutrality

The null differential outcome, ω, has been taken to locate the neutral point or affective zero of the affective scale. Outcomes preferred to ω are defined as desired and those to which ω is preferred as aversive. It is then an easy step to define *neutrality* and *neutral outcomes,* as follows.

> By definition, for all o, an organism *is neutral toward* an outcome, o, and o is a *neutral outcome*, if and only if $oI\omega$.   (4.11)

Note that neutrality, as defined here, is not the same as indifference but is a special case of it. To put it loosely, an organism that is indifferent between two outcomes does not care which one occurs, but the two outcomes may both be desired or both be aversive. On the other hand, an organism that is neutral toward some outcome may be said not to care whether it occurs or does not occur, and it is neither desired nor aversive. Common usage does not always preserve this distinction, but it will be adhered to strictly here.

Because preference is assumed to be transitive, under the stated restrictions, but indifference and its special case, neutrality, are taken to be nontransitive, three principles arise that may at first be surprising.

It is possible for an organism to be neutral to each of two
outcomes and yet to prefer one to the other.   (4.12)

Returning to the soft-drink example, (4.12) says that a child might be
neutral toward both Drink *a* and Drink *c*, but still prefer Drink *a* to
Drink *c*.

It is possible for an organism to desire some outcome and
yet to be indifferent between it and some neutral outcome.   (4.13)

Suppose that a child desires Drink *a* and is neutral toward Drink *b*. Then,
according to (4.13), the child may nevertheless be indifferent between the
two drinks.

It is possible for an organism to be neutral toward some
outcome and yet to be indifferent between it and some aversive
outcome.   (4.14)

If a child is neutral toward Drink *a* and aversive to Drink *b*, (4.14) states
that he may nevertheless be indifferent between the two drinks.

If the reader is disturbed by these principles, he should keep in mind
that they have less scope, the more sensitive the methods available for
testing preferences. They do, however, make it impossible to represent
indifference relations on the affective scale of Fig. 4.1; if two outcomes
between which an organism is indifferent were to be assigned to the same
point on the scale, indifference would have to be treated as transitive. In
other words, "ties" in a rank order of preference between pairs of
outcomes are not in general absolute, any more than an announced tie in a
footrace means that the runners arrived at the finish line with an
absolutely zero difference of time between them. The tie in the race
means merely that no difference was detected by the stopwatches or other
means employed for the determination. Principles (4.13) and (4.14) may
be thought of as illustrating a blurring of the boundaries between sets of
desired and neutral outcomes, and between sets of neutral and aversive
outcomes, a blurring that results from the nontransitivity of indifference.
The following principle holds, nevertheless:

No neutral outcome is preferred to any desired outcome,
and no neutral outcome is dispreferred to any aversive outcome.
                                                               (4.15)

This follows from the definitions. If, contrary to (4.15), some outcome were both neutral and at the same time preferred to some desired outcome, it would be preferred to ω, by (4.7) and (4.4), and not preferred to ω, by (4.11) and (3.1), which is a contradiction. Similarly, if an outcome were both neutral and at the same time dispreferred to some aversive outcome, it would be dispreferred to ω, by (4.8) and (4.5), and not dispreferred to ω, by (4.11) and (3.1), again a contradiction. This shows that the blurring introduced by the nontransitivity of indifference is far from unlimited in its scope.

CATEGORIES OF PREFERENCE AND INDIFFERENCE

The neutral point on the affective scale, represented by ω, was introduced in order to distinguish between outcomes that are pleasant, rewarding, or desired and those that are unpleasant, punishing, or aversive. The apparent qualitative difference between outcomes on the two sides of the scale would be neglected if the neutral point were eliminated and only quantitative differences in preference were preserved, as would be the case if, for example, one took Fig. 4.1 to represent no more than a rank order of eight outcomes (including ω). Suppose that you have won a contest and can choose between the prizes of a new automobile and a fully paid two-week trip to Paris; let the preferred prize be o_1 and the dispreferred prize be o_2 in the figure. Take Outcomes o_3, o_4, o_5, and o_6 to be other outcomes, which need not be specified, in the descending order of preference indicated in the figure. Finally, your life being eventful, imagine that you must choose between the continued severe pain of a disabled limb and the amputation of the limb, the preferred member of this pair being o_7 and the dispreferred, o_8, and that these two are at the bottom of the rank order as the figure indicates. If you believe that the difference between the preference values of the contest prizes and the preference values of the pain of the disabled limb and of its amputation are fully described as mere quantitative differences along a single homogeneous scale, you may regard the introduction of a neutral point as superfluous; but if not, you will welcome the classification of outcomes by means of the neutral point as useful and meaningful.

If desired, aversive, and neutral outcomes are defined as above and if preference is taken to be transitive and indifference as nontransitive, it turns out that the statement, "Outcome o is preferred to Outcome o'," may mean any one of exactly six things. To make it concrete, suppose that at some moment you prefer to spend the evening with Person A rather than with Person B. Calling these outcomes *a* and *b*, the possibilities are:

(1) both *a* and *b* are desired,
(2) *a* is desired and *b* is neutral,
(3) *a* is desired and *b* is aversive,
(4) both *a* and *b* are neutral (*cf*. (4.12)),
(5) *a* is neutral and *b* is aversive, and
(6) both *a* and *b* are aversive.

In the case of the statement, "The organism is indifferent between Outcomes *o* and *o'*," there are five possibilities. Continuing the example, but supposing that you are indifferent between spending the evening with Person A and spending it with Person B, the cases are:

(7) both *a* and *b* are desired,
(8) both *a* and *b* are neutral,
(9) both *a* and *b* are aversive,
(10) one of the two is desired and the other is neutral (*cf*. (4.13)), and
(11) one of the two is aversive and the other is neutral (*cf*. (4.14)).

It will be noted that Cases 4, 10, and 11 are due to the nontransitivity of indifference.

ACTS AS DESIRED OR AVERSIVE

If Act *a'* follows Act *a*, then *a'* is an outcome of *a*. It is therefore possible for acts, and opportunities to perform them, to be objects of preference and thus to be desired or aversive. Not to belabor an obvious point, see the later discussions of agonistic behavior in fish and mouse-killing in rats as possibly desired acts (Chapter 6, p. 81; Chapter 12, p. 168). Karsten's (1927) work on the development of strong aversiveness by acts that a human subject is required to repeat indefinitely ("over-satiation") affords interesting examples on the negative side. The error of taking the fact that one act occurs more frequently than another as sufficient evidence that it is preferred to the other must, however, be carefully avoided. (See the discussion of bias *vs*. preference in Chapter 3.) To show that an act is an object of preference requires its being observed as a differential outcome of the choice between some pair of acts of which it is not a member.

When acts are studied as outcomes, questions are likely to arise as to whether feedback and other immediate consequences of what the organism does are to be included in defining the acts. Such questions could hardly be avoided, for example, in such cases as a desire "to play tennis" or "to engage in sexual intercourse." It does not seem wise to try to lay down rules for deciding these issues outside the context of particular experimental and theoretical problems.

SUMMARY

By its empirical criteria, preference is an irreflexive and asymmetric binary relation, and by assumption it is also transitive. These properties hold for an organism at a particular moment, given constant c.p.f. and c.o.f. If ω is taken to locate a *neutral point*, an *affective scale* is established that amounts to a rank order of preference with two segments, one containing *desired outcomes*, *i.e.*, those that are preferred to ω, and the other containing *aversive outcomes*, *i.e.*, those are are dispreferred to ω. The state of preferring an outcome to ω is called *desire* for that outcome and that of preferring ω to an outcome is called *aversion* to that outcome.

If an organism prefers neither of two differential outcomes to the other, it is said to be *indifferent* between these outcomes. By its empirical criteria, indifference is a reflexive and symmetric binary relation at a given moment, with constant c.p.f. and c.o.f. Under these same restrictions it is assumed to be nontransitive.

An organism is said to be *neutral* toward an outcome if it is indifferent between that outcome and ω, and the outcome is called a *neutral outcome*. The nontransitivity of indifference produces a blurring that prevents this relation and its special case, neutrality, from being represented on the affective scale.

It follows from these definitions and assumptions that: (1) if Outcome o is desired and Outcome o' is aversive, then o is preferred to o'; (2) if o is preferred to o' and o' is desired, then o is desired; and (3) if o is aversive and is preferred to o', then o' is aversive; (4) no neutral outcome is preferred to any desired outcome; and (5) no neutral outcome is dispreferred to any aversive outcome. It also follows that instances of preference fall into six distinct classes and that instances of indifference fall into five distinct classes; these classes are enumerated in the text.

NOTES AND COMMENTS

1. Whether the intransitivities predicted and obtained in Tversky's (1969) ingenious experiments conflict fundamentally with the position taken here is not clear to the present writer. They appear to depend upon distinct differences from one decision to another in the subjects' attitudes toward the various objects of choice.

2. On problems having to do with the logical and mathematical properties of preference and indifference, and with scales of measurement of preference value ("utility"), see the fine chapter by Luce and Suppes (1965). A useful introduction to these problems is to be found in Coombs, Dawes, and Tversky (1970).

5

Act-Outcome Expectancies

Chapter 3 distinguished between behavior that depends upon the differential outcomes of the organism's acts and behavior that does not depend upon such outcomes. Thus, the criteria of preference and discrimination were said to be met only if the behavior is sensitive to its outcomes, whereas the criteria of bias and differential response do not require this. Although no act can be influenced by its own outcome, which is still in the future when the act is performed, the outcome of an act may affect later occurrences of acts of the same type. If Moos (Table 3.1) obtained food tokens when he opened the left panel and worthless tokens when he opened the right panel, in the presence of particular discriminanda, his later choices between these alternative acts might be, and indeed were, affected by these outcomes.

Consider now the trial when Moos was first introduced to Series II, in which the act that had formerly obtained the food token now obtained the worthless token. If he performed this act, thereby committing an unavoidable "error," it is not hard to imagine his showing signs of both surprise and anger at its outcome, which would be of some theoretical interest. The present point, however, has to do with the choice that Moos had just made. It would hardly be sensible to say that because he made a choice that got him a worthless token, he must have preferred such a token to a food token. Nor would it be reasonable to say that, since their father did not die, the children of Chapter 1 did not desire his death.[1]

It is clear that Moos preferred food tokens to worthless tokens on a trial in which his act produced the dispreferred token. How can such a preference be conceptualized without supposing that a future event may influence the present? The answer of a "cognitive" theory is that the organism prefers the outcome that it *expects* its act to produce; it prefers the actual outcome only if it coincides with this *expected outcome*. Moos expected a food token rather than a worthless token, and the children expected their father to be killed rather than to be saved. The fact that these expectancies were mistaken tells us, not that there are no such things as expectancies, but simply that they can be in error.

The task, then, is to discover how to diagnose expectancies and expected outcomes. The preceding discussion implies that choices depend upon two different kinds of organismic states, preferences and expectancies. Then, to put it loosely, if we know what an organism wants, its choices will tell us what it expects. For example, if a person chooses to enter Store A rather than Store B because at that moment he prefers buying a suit to buying a book, it is fair to conclude that he expects to get a suit by entering Store A rather than Store B. Or, if he dials one telephone number rather than another because he wishes to talk to a particular person, must he not expect calling this number, rather than the other, to result in his talking to that person? Such considerations suggest the form of a standard experiment for diagnosing what will be called "act-outcome expectancies."

THE DIAGNOSIS OF ACT-OUTCOME EXPECTANCIES

We take as an illustration an experiment by Kendler (1946), although his intentions in performing it were not the same as ours in analyzing it (as is true of many experiments that we cite). Kendler trained rats in a T-maze under both food and water deprivation, so that they were both hungry and thirsty. After the training trials he put the animals into the test situations shown in Table 5.1. Series I represents the test conditions and results of a subgroup that had always found food on the right and water on the left during training; Series II represents the test conditions and results of a subgroup that had always found water on the right and food on the left during training. The animals in these subgroups were further subdivided for the purposes of the four test trials; some were tested hungry but not thirsty, i.e., writing "f" for the outcome of eating food and "w" for that of drinking water, fPw (Conditions 1 and 1'), on Trials 1 and 4, and thirsty but not hungry, i.e., wPf (Conditions 2 and 2'), on Trials 2 and 3; the others were tested in the opposite order. The results show that a majority of the animals in each of the four subgroups turned on each trial to the side on which the outcome *that they now preferred* had always been found during the training trials. Specifically, the rats that now preferred food to water tended to turn to the right if food had been on the right during training (Series I) and to the left if food had been on the left (Series II), whereas the rats that now preferred water to food

Table 5.1
Act-outcome expectancies of rats in a T-maze
(Kendler, 1946)

	Conditions			
	Series I		Series II	
	1	2	1'	2'
	fPw	wPf	fPw	wPf
a_1: turns right	+ $o_1: f$	− $o_1: f$	− $o_2: w$	+ $o_2: w$
a_2: turns left	− $o_2: w$	+ $o_2: w$	+ $o_1: f$	− $o_1: f$

Note: Series I: food (f) on right, water (w) on left during training; Series II: food on left, water on right during training. The rats were trained under simultaneous food and water deprivation. Results are for test trials, under deprivation conditions presumed to result in fPw or wPf.

tended to turn to the left if water had been on the left in training (Series I) and to the right if water had been on the right (Series II).

We conclude from these results that the animals of Series I exhibited two *act-outcome expectancies*: namely, (1) that they would obtain food by turning right rather than by turning left and (2) that they would obtain water by turning left rather than by turning right. Similarly, the animals of Series II exhibited the act-outcome expectancies (1) that they would obtain water by turning right rather than by turning left and (2) that they would obtain food by turning left rather than by turning right. Note that these expectancies were acquired during the training trials, but that their existence was demonstrated by the results of the test trials.

Abstracting from particular preferences, acts, and outcomes, an experiment of the form of Table 5.1 will be called a *standard act-outcome expectancy experiment*, the form of which is shown in Table 5.2. In such an experiment, the organism is tested on any trial in one of two opposed preference states, oPo' and $o'Po$, to determine its choice between a pair of

Table 5.2
Form of the standard act-outcome expectancy experiment

	Conditions			
	Series I		Series II	
	1	2	1'	2'
	oPo'	$o'Po$	oPo'	$o'Po$
a	+ o	− o	− o'	+ o'
a'	− o'	+ o'	+ o	− o

Note: oPo' and $o'Po$ are opposed preferences; a and a' are alternative acts; o and o' are differential outcomes. Results such as are represented by the plus and minus signs would indicate that $aa'Eo$ and $a'aEo'$ in Series I and $aa'Eo'$ and $a'aEo$ in Series II.

alternative acts, a and a'. Controls against biases that link the acts differentially with the preference states may be necessary. Although it is unlikely in Kendler's experiment that the rats came to the procedure with biases to turn one way when hungry and the other when thirsty, biases would have been quite probable had he been observing, for example, their tendencies to salivate under the various conditions. The differences between the procedures of Series I and Series II provide controls against such biases. Given such controls, if the organism chooses Act a when oPo' and Act a' when $o'Po$, it may be said to exhibit the act-outcome expectancies (1) that a rather than a' will lead to o and (2) that a' rather than a will lead to o'.

The state of expecting to obtain Outcome o by Act a rather than by Act a' will be represented by the symbol $aa'Eo$. Outcome o in this symbol will be called the *expected outcome* of Act a. Using "r" for turning right and "l" for turning left, we can say of Kendler's rats in Series I, $rlEf$ and $lrEw$, and of those in Series II, $rlEw$ and $lrEf$. This merely puts in symbols what was said in English two paragraphs above.

As a second illustration, consider an experiment by Tolman and Gleitman (1949). Rats were run in a T-maze, two trials per day for nine days, under food deprivation. The goalboxes of the maze were distinguished by differences in color, lighting, shape, etc., but two pellets of food were present in each box. The first trial of each day was free; on the second trial, the subject was forced to the side opposite that of its choice on the free trial. Thus, the animals were given an opportunity to acquire the act-outcome expectancies (1) that they would find Box A by turning right rather than left and (2) that they would find Box B by turning left rather than right.

Test trials were then run to determine whether such expectancies would actually be exhibited. To induce the required opposed preference states, each animal was first given a series of severe electric shocks in one of the two boxes, which were at this time detached from the maze and placed in a different laboratory room, and then about two hours later was given a free trial in the maze. It will be supposed that animals shocked in Box B acquired a preference for Box A over Box B and that those shocked in Box A acquired a preference for Box B over Box A. Table 5.3 gives the conditions and results for the test trials, and shows that the animals did indeed turn to the side appropriate to these preferences. (This was true of 22 of the 25 subjects.)

Although Tolman and Gleitman did not run training trials with Box A on the left and Box B on the right, it is quite unlikely that the shocks in the two boxes happened to produce biases of just the sort required to give the obtained results. Consequently, we conclude that the rats exhibited two act-outcome expectancies, namely, (1) that they would find Box A by turning right rather than left, and (2) that they would find Box B by turning left rather than right. In symbols, *rlEa* and *lrEb*.

The reader may have observed that the differential outcomes indicated in the results cells of Table 5.3 (Tolman and Gleitman's experiment) are the *expected*, rather than the *actual*, outcomes of the subjects' choices. Because Tolman and Gleitman gave each animal only one test-trial, it was immaterial for the results whether or not the animals obtained the differential outcomes that they expected. It is for this reason that the symbols for the differential outcomes in this table are enclosed in parentheses. This was not done in Table 5.2, which shows the standard act-outcome expectancy experiment in abstract form, since it is perfectly possible to perform the experiment in one phase, instead of separating the acquisition and test phases as was done by Tolman and Gleitman. An example of this is an experiment by Leeper (1935), discussed in Chapter 9 and represented in Table 9.4, in which, after sufficient training, the

Table 5.3
Act-outcome expectancies of rats in a T-maze
(Tolman and Gleitman, 1949)

		Conditions	
		1	2
		aPb	bPa
a_1: turns right		+ o_1: (a)	− o_1: (a)
a_2: turns left		− o_2: (b)	+ o_2: (b)

Note: a and b are the differential outcomes of entering Goalboxes A and B; aPb and bPa are preferences presumed to have resulted from receiving shock in Boxes B and A, respectively, during training.

subjects both expected and obtained the differential outcomes of food or water. [Kendler (Table 5.1) used a mixed procedure; his animals had four test-trials in which they obtained food or water in its usual place.]

To bring this matter into clearer relief, a further illustration can be drawn from a somewhat more complex experiment by Irwin and Snodgrass (1966). In one of the procedures of this experiment, college students were required to bet from one to 10 cents against an equal amount on whether they would draw a marked card, *i.e.*, a card with an X on its face, or a blank card from a shuffled pack of 10 cards. Only one card was drawn from each pack. Packs with various numbers of marked and blank cards were used, and the subjects always knew the constitution of the pack from which they were about to draw. For simplicity, the illustration will deal only with packs that contained five marked and five blank cards.

The question at issue was whether subjects' expectancies of drawing, say, a marked card would be affected by the preference value of a marked card versus that of a blank card. To vary these preference values, drawing a marked card sometimes had positive money value (*e.g.*, +10 cents) and

Table 5.4
Act-outcome expectancies of college students
in a betting situation (Irwin and
Snodgrass, 1966)

	Conditions	
	1	2
	mPb	bPm
a_1: bets on m	+ o_1: (m)	− o_1: (m)
a_2: bets on b	− o_2: (b)	+ o_2: (b)

Note: m = marked card, b = blank card. mPb: m worth 10¢, b worth 0¢, regardless of bet; bPm: b worth 10¢, m worth 0¢, regardless of bet. The actual outcomes of a_1 and a_2 are m or b with probability .5 in each condition; the *expected* outcome of a_1 is m and that of a_2 is b, according to the interpretation given in the accompanying text.

sometimes had negative money value (*e.g.*, −10 cents), *regardless of the bet*; blank cards always had zero value.

Table 5.4 outlines these conditions. In Condition 1 it is supposed that the subjects preferred drawing a marked card to drawing a blank card (*i.e.*, mPb), since a marked card had positive money value, whereas in Condition 2, it is supposed that bPm, since a marked card had negative money value. Note that the *actual* outcomes of the draws in both conditions were marked or blank cards with probability .5; but the subjects were not informed of the results of their bets and draws until the experiment was over.

The results for the stated conditions are as indicated in the table. The subjects strongly tended to bet on a marked card when mPb and on a blank card when bPm. Although no reversal procedure was run (as would have been possible, for example, by having the subjects indicate bets on marked cards by pressing one of two keys in Series I and the other of the two keys in Series II), it seems safe to assume that such a reversal would have been successful. On that assumption, the results lead to the conclusion that a_1a_2Em and a_2a_1Eb. Thus, the subjects expected that betting on the preferred card (m in Condition 1 and b in Condition 2) rather than on the dispreferred card would lead to their obtaining the preferred card, even though they knew that equal numbers of the two kinds of cards were present in the packs. Such apparently irrational or "optimistic" expectancies have been found repeatedly under a variety of conditions (see references in Irwin and Snodgrass, 1966, and Irwin and Graae, 1968), but their interpretation is still in doubt.

Returning to the point of the illustration, observe that the expected outcome of Act a_1 is m and that of Act a_2 is b, whereas the actual outcomes of both acts are m or b with probability .5. Although the subjects in this experiment were given repeated trials, it could not matter to their later bets what cards they had actually drawn on earlier choices, since they were informed of this only when they had made all of their bets. As in the experiments of Kendler and of Tolman and Gleitman, the diagnosis of the subjects' expected outcomes depended, not upon the actual differential outcomes they obtained, but upon the differential outcomes that functioned as elements in the preferences controlling the choices. Thus, in the present illustration, m and b are taken to be the expected outcomes of Acts a_1 and a_2, respectively, because these acts are presumed to have been determined by the preferences mPb, in the first case, and bPm, in the second.

COMPLEMENTARY ACT-OUTCOME EXPECTANCIES

It was maintained above that the subjects of Kendler's Series I, those of his Series II, those of Tolman and Gleitman's experiment, and those of Irwin and Snodgrass's experiment each exhibited *two* act-outcome expectancies. For example, the subjects in Kendler's Series I were said to have shown the expectancies that they would obtain food by turning right rather than left and that they would obtain water by turning left rather than right. The standard act-outcome expectancy experiment is such that if a subject shows one such expectancy, it must also show another that is related to the first as $aa'Eo$ is related to $a'aEo'$, where a and a' are a pair of alternative acts, o and o' are a pair of differential outcomes, and the members of each pair are mutually exclusive and exhaustive. Act-outcome expectancies that are related in this way will be called *complementary*.

THE NATURE OF EXPECTANCIES

The notion of expectancy is central to "cognitive" theories, of which Tolman's (1932) is the classic example. It has frequently been criticized on the grounds that it is too ill-defined and that it leaves the organism's psychological states unconnected with action—even if Guthrie's quip about Tolman's leaving the rat buried in thought in the maze has by now become stale from frequent use, it still cannot be disregarded. (*Cf.* Miller, Galanter, and Pribram, 1960, p. 9ff.) However, the foregoing criteria of act-outcome expectancies, whatever else may be said about them, are definite enough to meet the former objection, and the reference of these expectancies to acts explicitly deals with the latter.

The conception of act-outcome expectancies as relations involving three terms, rather than just two, is essential to their role in the present system. An organism that displays the expectancy $aa'Eo$ is behaving as if it regarded the probability of obtaining Outcome o given that it performs Act a as being greater than the probability of its obtaining Outcome o given that it performs Act a'. It will be noted that this resembles, not an assertion of a probability, but an assertion that a likelihood ratio (a ratio of probabilities) is greater than one. Knowing that the organism expects a rather than a' to result in o tells us nothing about the probabilities that the organism would assign to o, given a *vs.* a', if it were capable of such an assignment, except that the former would be greater than the latter. Both might be large, both might be small, or the former might be large and the latter small. It is particularly important to remember this when, given $aa'Eo$, o is spoken of as the *expected outcome* of a. This expression does not imply that the organism is implicitly judging the probability of o, given a, to be greater than .5; it merely implies that the organism acts as if it took this probability to be greater than that of the same outcome, given a'. More precisely, then, o should be called the *expected outcome of a rather than a'*, but for brevity the latter part of the phrase will be omitted as understood.

Sources of Uncertainty

An organism's uncertainty as to which of two acts is the more likely to lead to a particular outcome may arise from at least two different sources. First, outcomes may be related to acts probabilistically. Although no experimental examples of this have been described in this chapter, cases are numerous both in experiment and in ordinary experience. An experimenter might arrange to put food in the left box of a T-maze on a random 80% of the trials and in the right box, independently, on a random 50% of the trials, the alternative to food in each case being ω. Brunswik (1939) performed perhaps the earliest experiments of this sort.

In such a case, food is more likely to be obtained by a left turn than by a right turn, and Brunswik's rats apparently were able to learn differential expectancies accordingly. It is also possible, of course, for an organism to believe that acts and outcomes are related probabilistically when in fact they are not.

Second, an organism may be uncertain as to which of two acts leads to which of two differential outcomes even though the outcomes are not probabilistically related to the acts and are not regarded as being so. For example, a novice oarsman knows that pulling on one oar turns the boat in one direction and pulling the other turns it in the other direction, but he may be doubtful as to which oar to pull to turn in the desired direction. Such situations are frequent in the lives of persons who have chronic difficulty in identifying "right" and "left." Similarly, one may know that a young woman is either Miss Smith or Miss Jones, and yet not know by which name to address her. It seems reasonable to suppose that it is largely this kind of uncertainty that is gradually overcome by a rat as it learns which side of a maze has food in it and which does not, when one and only one side always does contain food. Of course, both sources of uncertainty may be present, as was probably true, for instance, in at least the early learning trials of Brunswik's experiments with probabilistic food rewards in a maze.

Expectancies of Types Other Than aa'Eo

Several types of expectancy other than $aa'Eo$ can be conceived of, although their empirical criteria have not yet been established. They are undoubtedly essential to the understanding of various psychological problems, including, for example, those of acquired motivation. Each is a three-term relation.

1. Type $aEoo'$. An organism may have an expectancy that Act a is more likely to lead to Outcome o than to Outcome o'. For example, one of Brunswik's rats might expect that turning right is more likely to lead to food than to ω; or a person might expect that a soft answer is more likely to turn away wrath than to aggravate it. Expectancies of this sort would be represented by the symbol $aEoo'$. It might at first be thought that the existence of such an expectancy could be derived from the existence of the complementary pair, $aa'Eo$ and $a'aEo'$; but that this is mistaken has already been pointed out in the discussion of expected outcomes. The rat might regard food as more likely if it turns right than if it turns left, and ω as more likely if it turns left than it it turns right, without regarding

food as more likely than ω in either case. This would in fact be justified if, for example, food was placed on the right in 40 percent of the trials at random and, independently, on the left in 20 percent of the trials at random. Similarly, a soft answer to a highly aggrieved opponent might be more likely to turn away his wrath than a sharp response, and still have little chance of succeeding. It is clear that the criteria of $aa'Eo$ and $a'aEo'$ do not suffice for $aEoo'$.

2. Types $ee'Ee''$ and $eEe'e''$. It can hardly be doubted that human beings and some other organisms are capable of acquiring expectancies that link together occurrences among events other than acts and outcomes, which may be called *event-event expectancies*. The expectancy that an overcast sky rather than sunshine will be followed by rain, or that a buzzer rather than a flashing light will be followed by an electric shock, would be represented by the symbol $ee'Ee''$, with e specified as "overcast" or "buzzer," e' as "sunshine" or "flashing light," and e'' as "rain" or "electric shock." The expectancy that overcast will be followed by rain rather than snow, or that a buzzer will be followed by shock rather than ω, would be represented by $eEe'e''$, with the obvious specifications. Scientific facts and laws permit human beings to form infinitely many event-event expectancies of all degrees of complexity and quantitative precision.

LOGICAL PROPERTIES OF ACT-OUTCOME EXPECTANCIES

The relation $aa'Eo$ is a state of an organism and, like preferences, discriminations, and other psychological states, is not a permanent property of the organism but changes during the course of time under the influence of variables the discovery of which is a principal task of psychology. For a given organism at a given time, and holding constant the c.p.f., the c.o.f., and the expected outcome, we assume that act-outcome expectancies are irreflexive, asymmetric, and transitive with respect to the acts.

As to their being irreflexive, the standard act-outcome experiment obviously cannot lead to the meaningless conclusion that an organism expects a particular act to be more likely than itself to have a given outcome. In symbols: for all a, a', and o,

$$\sim(aaEo). \qquad (5.1)$$

As to their being asymmetric with respect to the acts, it follows from the standard act-outcome expectancy experiment that, for example, a rat cannot be found simultaneously to expect that turning right rather than left will get it food and to expect that turning left rather than right will get it food. In symbols: for all a, a', and o,

$$aa'Eo \rightarrow \sim(a'aEo). \tag{5.2}$$

The converse of (5.2) does not, of course, necessarily hold. Knowledge that the rat does *not* expect to get food by turning right rather than left does not permit the conclusion that it expects to get food by turning left rather than right. First, the animal may have no expectancy at all with respect to this outcome and these acts; but even if it does, it may regard the outcome as equally likely, whichever act is performed.

As to the transitivity of act-outcome expectancies over available acts at a given moment, this means, for example, that if being noticed by a taxicab driver is expected to result from shouting at the driver rather than from waving at him, and if the same outcome is expected to result from waving at him rather than from looking wistful, then the outcome is expected to result from shouting at him rather than looking wistful. In symbols: for all a, a', a'', and o,

$$(aa'Eo \land a'a''Eo) \rightarrow aa''Eo. \tag{5.3}$$

It is worth noting that (5.3) implies nothing about the effectiveness of *combinations* of acts in obtaining a given outcome unless these combinations are treated as single acts. Thus, it would not be correct to conclude from the hypotheses of the example that the person expects the combination of shouting and waving to be more likely to catch the driver's attention than merely looking wistful (or than merely shouting or merely waving). The facts do not tell us whether or not he had such an expectancy. (Nor is it obvious that a combination of acts would actually be more successful than one of the acts singly—the driver might be annoyed by the prospective passenger's overeagerness.)

If we hold the acts constant and vary the outcome, other possibilities arise. Suppose that calling a friend on the telephone rather than refraining from calling him is expected to lead to a pleasant conversation, and that calling rather than refraining from calling is also expected to lead to an invitation to a party. Then we shall assume that calling rather than refraining from calling is expected to lead to the combined outcome of a pleasant conversation and an invitation to a party. In symbols: for all a, a', o, and o',

$$(aa'Eo \land aa'Eo') \rightarrow aa'E(o, o'). \tag{5.4}$$

The principle is intended to hold equally for any number of outcomes. Its converse, however, cannot be assumed: that is, the fact that a combination of two or more outcomes is expected to result from one act rather than another does not necessarily imply that each of the outcomes taken singly is expected to result from the former act rather than the latter. In a choice between two jobs, for example, a person might regard the combination of good pay and an easy life as more likely if he accepted Job X than if he accepted Job Y. At the same time, he might regard accepting Job Y, rather than Job X, as more likely to result in good pay but not an easy life, or in an easy life without good pay. It is even possible for the probabilities of good pay and an easy life in Job Y *both* to be higher, taken singly, than the probability of their combination in Job X, although the probability of the combination is higher in Job X than in Job Y. (Consider, for example, the case in which the two outcomes are positively correlated in Job X and negatively correlated in Job Y.) If so, there is no reason why the person's expectancies should not reflect such a state of affairs. Consequently, the fact that the person expects to obtain the combination of good pay and an easy life by accepting Job X rather than Job Y does not imply that he regards this choice as more likely than the other to get him *either* good pay or an easy life.

SUMMARY

Concepts of expectancy are central to cognitive psychological theories. Empirical criteria in the form of a standard experiment were offered for one such concept, that of *act-outcome expectancies*. These criteria require that the organism be tested under each of two opposed preference states and that it choose one of two alternative acts in one state and the other in the other state. Positive results demonstrate that the organism has an expectancy of the form $aa'Eo$, where the symbol may be read, "The organism expects to obtain Outcome o by performing Act a rather than Act a'." In such a case, Outcome o is called the *expected outcome* of Act a.

The formal properties of $aa'Eo$ as a three-term relation were discussed. The presumable existence of other types of expectancies, such as would be represented by $aEoo'$ and (using "e" for events other than acts and outcomes) by $ee'Ee''$ and $eEe'e''$ was noted, but criteria of them have not been established.

NOTES AND COMMENTS

1. Freud's (1938) account of mistakes, slips of the tongue, accidents, and other lapses, together with the trend of his whole theory, has

often led to interpretations of behavior no less absurd than to claim that the children really (*i.e.*, unconsciously) did not want their father to die and (except that animals would be excluded from the theory) that Moos did want a worthless token. Taking observed outcomes of acts as signs of what was unconsciously desired makes anyone an instant psychologist. Although Freud himself allowed for the operation of chance in the external world, he can hardly be absolved of all responsibility for such crude excesses. (See also the discussion of unintended consequences of intentional acts in Chapter 7.)

2. The nature of the standard act-outcome experiment is such that positive results necessarily demonstrate the existence not only of one expectancy, but also of another that is complementary to it. Thus, if we have evidence that a rat expects to obtain food by turning right rather than by turning left, the same evidence tells us that the rat expects to obtain some other outcome by turning left rather than right. In general, if an organism expects to obtain a particular outcome by performing one act rather than another, then there is some other outcome that the organism expects to obtain by performing the latter act rather than the former. In symbols: for any a and a',

$$(\exists o)aa'Eo \;\;\leftrightarrow\;\; (\exists o')a'aEo'. \tag{5.5}$$

Note that the unspecified nature of o and o' in (5.5) is significant. It means, for example, that, if we wish to test for $aa'Eo$, we are free to choose o' as we like. If we want to know whether a rat has the expectancy that it will obtain food by turning right rather than left, we can use preference states involving food *vs.* water or food *vs.* sex or food *vs.* electric shock, or whatever is most convenient or enlightening.

In this context, consider experiments on "imitation." To find out whether a child expects to obtain a piece of candy by copying a model rather than by doing something else, we may use the child's preference between the candy and a toy, a trinket, an empty box, or any other differential outcome as the state to be varied. In such an experiment we are likely to be interested in the generality of the expectancies that have been formed. For example, we might wish to know whether the child has acquired the expectancies that he will obtain *whatever the model obtained* by copying the model rather than by not doing so, and that he will obtain *an outcome other than what the model obtained* if he performs the alternative act rather than copying the model. To test for such generalized expectancies, we would use a number of pairs of differential outcomes differing from each other along many dimensions, under the restriction that we know in advance which member of each pair is preferred to the other. Alternatively, we might wish to diagnose more precisely the features of the model's acts that are critical for the subject's expectancies concerning his own acts. Here, the concomitant variation between the details of the model's behavior and that of the subject would be the object of study. The acts chosen by the subject, and the relations between them and the acts performed by the model, would permit us to specify more and more narrowly both what acts are involved in his act-outcome expectancies and what features of the model's behavior he is actually copying. The latter goes toward the problem of discovering how the subject "perceives" the behavior of the model.

3. Fractional anticipatory goal responses—the r_g–s_g mechanisms—in neo-Hullian theory are commonly taken to be the functional counterpart of expectancies in cognitive theory. Deutsch (1956) has shown how easily an S–R theorist can slip from consistency in the use of these mechanisms by attributing to them unwarranted properties borrowed from the cognitive analogy. Aside from this difficulty, as well as those that arise from the unhappy lack of independent criteria, a fractional goal response refers to only one act, whereas act-outcome expectancies refer to two; it is consequently impossible for a single r_g–s_g to have the same properties as $aa'Eo$. If the reader wishes to attempt to construct act-outcome expectancies from pairs of r_g–s_g mechanisms and make them fit the standard act-outcome expectancy experiment, while at the same time remaining faithful to some S–R view of learning, he is welcome to the task. Four such mechanisms will be needed for Series I of the experiment and four others for Series II. Similar comments apply to the formalization of expectancy by MacCorquodale and Meehl (1953), even though their views were persuasive to Tolman, as can be seen in his late survey of his system (Tolman, 1959); *cf.* Irwin (1966).

4. The reversal of preference required by the standard act-outcome expectancy experiment as described above is not necessarily easy to achieve in practice. Although Kendler (Table 5.1) was able to make his rats prefer food to water or water to food on particular trials, as desired, it nevertheless required such spacing of trials as would provide for the periods of deprivation of water and food. Other cases might be more difficult, as, for example, that in which the expected outcomes to a child were a toy for one act and a piece of candy for the alternative act; the experimenter would be hard-pressed to arrange for the child to prefer toy to candy on specified random trials and candy to toy on the other trials.

Ingenuity is often required to circumvent such difficulties. In many cases the reversal of preferences can be achieved by establishing contingent preferences between the outcomes under study and some pair of differential outcomes whose relative preference values for the organism are known and sufficiently definite. Nothing is more common in decision-making experiments than just this. It may be a matter of indifference to S whether a coin toss emerges as "heads" or "tails" or a drawn card is marked or blank or a key press produces a buzz or silence until he learns that money gains and losses are associated with these events. The criteria of expectancies given here require that S have preferences between the outcomes, but they do not require that these preferences be in some way intrinsic to the outcomes. No one (or, at any rate, no cognitively disposed psychologist) can doubt that Wolfe's (1936) chimpanzees formed various expectancies in which poker chips were the expected outcomes, but it is equally clear that the values of these tokens were formed by differential association with food, water, play, and other outcomes whose own values had a history that could only be surmised. [Most of this paragraph is quoted from an earlier discussion (Irwin, 1966, pp. 329-330).]

Tolman and Gleitman's experiment (Table 5.3) is another instance of this. It will be recalled that, in this experiment, some animals were given electric shock in Box A and not in Box B, while some where shocked in Box B but not in Box A. The test trials, as interpreted here, involved preferences between entering Box A and entering Box B, and, by the same interpretation, the expectancies that were exhibited by the animals had the expected outcomes of entering one or the other of these boxes. But if Tolman and Gleitman had wished to demonstrate expectancies in which the expected outcomes were electric shock and ω, the present criteria would have required them to make the shock sometimes aversive and sometimes desired, an unappealing task.

5. Experiments on "latent learning," of which the studies by Kendler (Table 5.1) and Tolman and Gleitman (Table 5.3) are examples, commonly consist of two phases, a training phase in which the subject is given an opportunity to acquire certain act-outcome expectancies and a test phase in which the subject can exhibit these expectancies if it has acquired them. [For reviews of such experiments, see, e.g., Thistlethwaite (1951) and Kimble (1961).] If the test phase is adequate, the experiments show whether or not the subject acquired the expectancies for which an opportunity was given, and thus throw light on the conditions that bring about the acquisition of such expectancies. The views just expressed are somewhat different from the attitudes of theorists during the polemical stage of learning theory from, say, 1930 to 1950, when it was hoped that the results of single crucial experiments might decide between "cognitive" and "reinforcement" positions.

6

Intentional Act,
Intended Outcome, and Choice

With experimental criteria of preference and act-outcome expectancy at hand, it is possible to construct definitions of the concepts *intentional act, intended outcome, chosen act,* and *chosen outcome.* We begin with three hypothetical illustrations, each of which will be referred to frequently.

1. A child is confronted by two boxes, one blue and one yellow. If he opens the blue box, and if the occurrence of this act depends upon (1) his preferring a toy to a trinket, (2) his expecting to obtain a toy by opening the blue box rather than the yellow one, and (3) his expecting to obtain a trinket by opening the yellow box rather than the blue one, then he will be said to have *chosen* the act of opening the blue box over that of opening the yellow box and the outcome of obtaining a toy over the outcome of obtaining a trinket. His act will be called *intentional* and the toy will be called its *intended outcome.*

2. If a subject says "yes" in a particular trial in a signal-detection experiment, and if this act depends upon (1) his preference for winning 5¢ over losing 5¢, (2) his expecting that saying "yes" rather than saying "no" will result in his winning 5¢, and (3) his expecting that saying "no" rather than saying "yes" will result in his losing 5¢, then he has chosen the act of saying "yes" over that of saying "no" and the outcome of winning 5¢ over that of losing 5¢. Saying "yes" was intentional and had the intended outcome of winning 5¢.

3. If a dog jumps a hurdle from one side of a box to the other, and if this act depends upon (1) its being averse to shock, (2) its expecting to obtain ω by jumping rather than refraining from jumping, and (3) its expecting to receive shock by refraining from jumping rather than jumping, then it has chosen the act of jumping over that of refraining from jumping and the outcome ω over that of shock. The act of jumping was intentional and its intended outcome was ω.

74

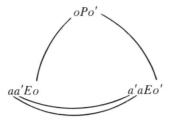

Fig. 6.1. An interlocked triad

The triad is composed of a preference, oPo', and a pair of complementary act-outcome expectancies, $aa'Eo$ and $a'aEo'$. Identical elements are indicated by lines that connect them. Note that each element is identical to exactly one other element. Note also that o, the preferred member of the pair of outcomes, is also the expected outcome of Act a, and that o', the dispreferred member of the pair of outcomes, is also the expected outcome of Act a'. In behavior determined by this triad, the chosen act would be a and the rejected alternative act would be a'.

INTERLOCKED TRIADS

The chosen act in each illustration depended upon three states of the organism, a preference and a pair of complementary act-outcome expectancies. These three states involved in each case only a single pair of alternative acts and a single pair of differential outcomes; the preferred outcome was also the expected outcome of the chosen act, and the dispreferred outcome was the expected outcome of the rejected alternative act; and both expectancies referred to the same pair of alternative acts. In such cases, if a is the chosen act, a' the rejected alternative act, o the preferred outcome, and o' the dispreferred outcome, the three states may be represented by oPo', $aa'Eo$, and $a'aEo'$, and constitute what will be called an *interlocked triad*. (Such a triad is represented in Fig. 6.1.) In Illustration 1, a is opening the blue box, a' is opening the yellow box, o is obtaining a toy, and o' is obtaining a trinket. The chosen act of opening the blue box depended upon the interlocked triad made up of (1) oPo', the preference for a toy over a trinket, (2) $aa'Eo$, the expectancy that a toy would be obtained by opening the blue box rather than the yellow one, and (3) $a'aEo'$, the expectancy that a trinket would be obtained by opening the yellow box rather than the blue one. A similar analysis can be applied straightforwardly to Illustrations 2 and 3.

EMPIRICAL DEPENDENCE

It is often necessary, as in the illustrations, to assert that the occurrence of an act depends empirically upon certain preferences and expectancies. The relation of empirical dependence will be represented by an asterisk or "star." Thus, "a $*$ oPo'" may be read, "The occurrence of Act a depends upon a preference for Outcome o over Outcome o'," or, equivalently, "A preference for Outcome o over Outcome o' is necessary for the occurrence of Act a."

No analysis or axiomatization of this dependence relation is known to the writer and none will be attempted here, but instances of it are familiar in the various sciences and their applications. The occurrence of certain chemical reactions depends upon the presence of a catalyst; the appearance of a picture on a television screen depends upon the elements of the picture tube attaining a certain temperature; in many animal species, conception depends upon the union of male and female germ cells; a nuclear explosion depends upon the presence of a critical mass; etc., etc. In each case, the dependence is a matter of one event or state being necessary under a given set of circumstances for the occurrence of another. This resembles the logical concept of material implication, in which the statement, "$p \rightarrow q$," i.e., "p materially implies q," means that p is true only if q is true. Empirical dependence, however, deals with factual, not merely logical, considerations. In particular, in logic, if p and q are both true, then p implies q and q implies p. But clearly we do not want this to hold in the dependence relation, since it would lead to our taking mere coincidences for empirical dependencies. For example, if it happens that it is raining and that an experimental rat turns to the right in a T-maze, we do not wish to conclude from this that the rat's act depended upon the rain (nor, for that matter, that the rain depended upon the rat's act). We shall therefore make the following assumptions about the dependence relation. Taking p and q to be assertions of the occurrence of observable events, we assume, first, that:

$$(p * q) \rightarrow (p \rightarrow q). \tag{6.1}$$

That is, if p empirically depends upon q, then p only if q. For example, if "$a * oPo'$" is true, then we can conclude from an occurrence of Act a that "oPo'" is true.

Second, because we do not wish to conclude from the mere coincidence of two events that one empirically depends upon the other, we assume that:

$$\text{even if ``}p \wedge q\text{'' is true, ``}p * q\text{'' may be false.} \qquad (6.2)$$

For example, Act a may occur and the organism may at the same time prefer o to o', and yet the act may not empirically depend upon the preference; that is, if both "a" and "oPo'" are true, "a $*$ oPo'" may nevertheless be false.

Third, if one event materially implies another, the former does not necessarily depend empirically upon the latter. That is:

$$\text{even if ``}p \to q\text{'' is true, ``}p * q\text{'' may be false.} \qquad (6.3)$$

This follows from (6.2) and the logical truth that "$p \wedge q$" implies "$p \to q$." Thus, if for reasons of coincidence or any other reasons an occurrence of Act a materially implies a preference for o over o', we cannot necessarily conclude that the act empirically depends upon the preference; "a $\to$ oPo'" may be true and "a $*$ oPo'" may nevertheless be false.

Finally, because an event often depends empirically upon two or more other events, it will be convenient to assume that:

$$(p * q) \wedge (p * r) \leftrightarrow [p * (q \wedge r)]. \qquad (6.4)$$

For example, if Act a empirically depends upon oPo' and also upon $aa'Eo$, then it depends upon the conjunction of oPo' and $aa'Eo$, and conversely, so that "(a $*$ oPo') $\wedge$ (a $*$ $aa'Eo$)" and "a $*$ ($oPo' \wedge aa'Eo$)" mean the same thing.

It is important to keep in mind two facts about the relation of empirical dependence. First, it is intended to relate only propositions that are definitionally independent of each other. For example, the statement, "Outcome o is desired," does not depend empirically upon the statement, "Outcome o is preferred to ω," since the truth of the former statement depends by definition (4.4) upon the truth of the latter. Second, assertions of empirical dependence usually, perhaps always, hold only under particular surrounding conditions; it is a familiar fact that the temperature required for water to boil can be specified, but only for a given pressure. In what follows, the truth of such a statement as, for example, "a $*$ oPo'," will generally be subject to the existence of very special circumstances of an experiment or of a hypothetical real-life situation.

INTENTIONAL ACT, INTENDED OUTCOME, CHOSEN ACT, AND CHOSEN OUTCOME

Intentional Act

Given the concepts of interlocked triad and empirical dependence, the way to a definition of intentional acts is clear. To abstract from the illustrations, we take an act to be intentional if and only if its occurrence depends upon the existence of an interlocked triad in which the expected outcome of the act in question is also the preferred outcome and the expected outcome of the alternative act is also the dispreferred outcome. In Illustration 1, the child's act of opening the blue box is intentional because its occurrence depends upon just such a triad: the expected outcome of this act is a toy, which is also the preferred outcome, and the expected outcome of the alternative act of opening the yellow box is a trinket, which is also the dispreferred outcome. In Illustration 2, the expected outcome of the intentional act of saying "yes" is 5¢, which is also the preferred outcome, and the expected outcome of saying "no" is the loss of 5¢, which is also the dispreferred outcome. In Illustration 3, the expected outcome of the intentional act of jumping is ω, which is also the preferred outcome, while the expected outcome of refraining from jumping is receiving electric shock, which is also the dispreferred outcome.

The formal definition of *intentional act* may be given as follows, using "Ia" to mean "Act a is intentional": by definition, for any act, a,

$$Ia \leftrightarrow [a * (\exists a') (\exists o) (\exists o') (oPo' \wedge aa'Eo \wedge a'aEo')]. \tag{6.5}$$

This definition may be read, "By definition, Act a is intentional if and only if its occurrence depends upon a preference for some differential outcome, o, over another differential outcome, o', upon an expectancy that o will result from a rather than from some alternative act, a', and upon an expectancy that o' will result from a' rather than a."

Intended Outcome

Parallel to this is the definition of the *intended outcome of an act*. Reading "Io_a" as "Outcome o is the intended outcome of Act a," we have: by definition, for any outcome, o, and act, a,

$$Io_a \leftrightarrow [a * (\exists a') (\exists o') (oPo' \wedge aa'Eo \wedge a'aEo')]. \tag{6.6}$$

That is: "By definition, Outcome o is the intended outcome of Act a if and only if the occurrence of Act a depends upon a preference for o over some other differential outcome, o', upon an expectancy that a rather than some alternative act, a', will lead to o, and upon an expectancy that a' rather than a will lead to o'."

It may be repeated here from Note 2, Chapter 1, that the term "intended outcome," as defined here, qualifies as one of the numerous meanings of the word "purpose" in common usage.

Chosen Act

Embodied in the definition of an intentional act are references to an alternative act, and the illustrations have freely employed the notion, explicitly or implicitly, that when an intentional act occurs, it has been chosen over such an alternative. We take the concept of *choice* to refer to whatever process eventuates in the occurrence of one of the two alternative acts. Reading "Ca" as "Act a is chosen," we state: by definition, for any act, a,

$$Ca \leftrightarrow Ia \wedge a. \tag{6.7}$$

This may be read, "By definition, Act a is chosen if and only if it is intentional and it occurs." The alternative act, a', to which this definition implicitly refers, may be called the *rejected act*, and a may be said to have been *chosen over a'*.

Chosen Outcome

Similarly, the intended outcome of a chosen act may be thought of as having been chosen over the expected outcome of the rejected act. Taking "Co_a" as "Outcome o is the chosen outcome of Act a," we have: by definition, for any outcome, o, and any act, a,

$$Co_a \leftrightarrow Io_a \wedge a. \tag{6.8}$$

This may be read: "By definition, Outcome o is the chosen outcome of Act a if and only if Act a occurs and Outcome o is its intended outcome."

Equivalences

These definitions imply that if an act is intentional, it has an intended outcome, and, conversely, that if the outcome of an act is intended, the act is intentional. This may be written: for all a,

$$Ia \leftrightarrow (\exists o)Io_a. \tag{6.9}$$

Similarly, the definitions of chosen act and chosen outcome imply that whenever an organism chooses, it chooses both an act and an outcome. More formally, if an act is chosen, it has a chosen outcome and, conversely, if an outcome is the chosen outcome of an act, then that act itself is chosen. This may be written: for all a,

$$Ca \leftrightarrow (\exists o)Co_a. \tag{6.10}$$

Incompleteness of the System

The system presented here is incomplete in many ways. In particular, although by Definition (6.5) the existence of an interlocked triad is necessary for the occurrence of an intentional act, the act may not occur even if the triad exists. Suppose one knows that a child will open a blue box only if it prefers a toy to a trinket and if it expects to get a toy by opening the blue box rather than a yellow one and if it expects to get a trinket rather than a toy by opening the yellow box rather than the blue one; this qualifies the act of opening the blue box as intentional. Suppose one knows, in addition, that the preference and complementary expectancies just described actually exist in the child at a particular time. Then it is still not possible to infer that the child will open the blue box. For example, the box might in fact not be present; if present, it might be hidden; if not hidden, it might for other reasons not be perceived; a conflict might exist that was resolved in favor of another act; and so on. These considerations suggest their own remedies and do not prevent predictions from being made for tests of hypotheses or for practical purposes. Intentional acts do occur; and if they occur, their sufficient conditions must have been present, whether they are known or not.

INTENTIONAL AND NONINTENTIONAL ACTS

Psychologists seem to understand each other fairly well when they use the adjectives "intentional" or "voluntary," even in the absence of adequate definition of these words. (See, for example, Kimble and Perlmuter, 1970.) This understanding rests in part upon the explicit or implicit acceptance of motivational and cognitive criteria resembling those employed here.[5] Acts that are "stimulus bound" or are otherwise unresponsive to variation in their outcomes, such as reflexes, Pavlovian conditioned responses, orienting behavior (taxes), highly specific "instinctive" responses, and automatized habits are usually treated as nonintentional or nonvoluntary, and debate in particular instances is likely to center upon evaluation of evidence rather than upon the underlying criteria themselves. Overlapping between our intentional acts and Skinner's "operants" is clear in the case of "discriminated operants" (Skinner, 1938), although the latter might include habitual acts so automatized that they no longer depended upon an interlocked triad. The case of unconditioned operants is difficult, and no judgment on their status will be offered here. Finally, it may be remarked that the acquisition and modification of act-outcome expectancies, which is required by our criteria, is obviously a form of learning; organisms that are incapable of such learning, of which the blowfly is apparently an example (Dethier, 1964), are unlikely to exhibit behavior that one is tempted to call intentional.

In the case of instinctive behavior, it is important to distinguish sharply between the instinctive acts themselves and other acts that may have the function of providing the opportunity for the instinctive acts and their consequences to occur. For example, according to Myer and White (1965), rats choose the arm of a T-maze that leads to the opportunity of killing a mouse over the arm that leads to the (unused) opportunity of killing a rat pup. This behavior appears to be intentional and to have the intended outcome of the act of mouse-killing or something closely associated therewith, but the mouse-killing act itself may be instinctive and nonintentional. (A rat can hardly be thought to intend the *death* of a mouse; "mouse-killing" is the observer's name for a complex outcome of which he does not know the psychologically effective features. This will be discussed further in Chapter 11.) As another example, Thompson (1963) has shown that Siamese fighting fish (*Betta splendens*) will learn to swim through a ring in an aquarium if doing so gives them the opportunity to display an agonistic response to their own image in a mirror or to a colored model of a male of their species. It would be interesting to know whether the effective outcome is the sight of the male image or model, the act of making the agonistic display, some unidentified outcome associated with the sight or the act, or a combination of these. It may be noted that Peterson (1960) was able to train young ducklings to peck a key that

illuminated a moving yellow cylinder upon which they had been imprinted and even, apparently, to refrain from pecking the key if this was
made necessary for the outcome; but the act of "following" the imprinted
object seems not to have been necessary for the learning.

Rejected Acts Are Intentional.

It was pointed out that the definition of a chosen act refers to an
alternative act over which the act that occurred was chosen, and this is
called the *rejected act*. We now assume that *every such rejected act is an
intentional act*. In the illustrations at the beginning of this chapter, this
assumption will perhaps seem reasonable enough if the child chooses to
open the blue box, and in so doing rejects the act of opening the yellow
box; the latter act is obviously capable of being chosen on another similar
occasion, given an appropriate change in the child's preference or expectancies, and is therefore intentional. The same holds for the signal-
detection experiment; if the subject says "yes" on a particular trial and
thereby rejects the act of saying "no," on other trials of the same
experiment his expectancies would be such as to result in his saying "no"
and rejecting saying "yes." Likewise, the dog that chooses to jump the
hurdle in the two-compartment box to avoid shock, and thus rejects the
act of refraining from jumping, might be trained to refrain from jumping
and thus to reject the act of jumping; this "passive avoidance" would
indicate that refraining from jumping is intentional. Recall that the
standard preference and expectancy experiments require the organism to
perform both of the relevant alternative acts, one under some conditions
and the other under others.

It may be objected, however, that there are instances in which an
intentional act is chosen over a *nonintentional* act such as coughing,
sneezing, weeping, going to sleep, or the like. Might one not refrain from
coughing during a quiet passage at an orchestra concert, or refrain from
weeping at a sentimental scene in a motion picture? Might one not choose
to take part in the conversation at a late party rather than go to sleep in
public? From the present point of view, one might indeed do each of
these things, to the extent to which he has control over the opposing
tendency; but then the rejected alternative act needs to be classified
differently than it would be if no choice were involved. If a choice is made
between coughing and not coughing, the alternatives may properly be
spoken of as "refraining from coughing" and "permitting oneself to
cough." The same holds for sneezing, weeping, and going to sleep. It is not
meaningless to say, "I permitted myself the luxury of crying," or, "I

allowed myself to show my anger," no matter how subtle or difficult it may be to distinguish between these cases and those of uncomplicated displays of reflexive or emotional acts. The problem is to determine whether or not the act depends upon some interlocked triad; that determination may not be easy, but the question is nonetheless a factual one.

SUMMARY

The terms *intentional act, intended outcome, chosen act,* and *chosen outcome* are defined by means of the concepts of *empirical dependency* and *interlocked triad*. Empirical dependency is a relation such that the occurrence of an event requires the occurrence of another event or state. An interlocked triad is constituted of a preference and a pair of complementary act-outcome expectancies such that the preferred outcome is the expected outcome of one of a pair of alternative acts, and the dispreferred outcome is the expected outcome of the other alternative act. An intentional act, then, is an act the occurrence of which depends upon the existence of an interlocked triad in which the act in question has the preferred outcome as its expected outcome. An intended outcome of an act is just such an expected and preferred outcome. A chosen act is an act that is intentional and that occurs; and the chosen outcome of an act is the intended outcome of that chosen act. It follows from these definitions that every intentional act has an intended outcome, and that if an outcome is the intended outcome of an act, then the act is intentional. Similarly, every chosen act has a chosen outcome, and if an outcome is the chosen outcome of an act, then that act is chosen. The present system is far from complete; in particular, the occurrence of an act cannot be inferred from the facts that the act is intentional and that the members of the interlocked triad upon which its occurrence depends exist.

Classes of acts that are not expected to meet the criteria of intentional and chosen acts are those commonly referred to as reflexes, Pavlovian conditioned reflexes, taxes, instinctive acts, and automatized habits.

NOTES AND COMMENTS

1. The term "intentional act" was chosen over "voluntary act" because the relation represented by *Ia* appeared to be closer to the common-speech meaning of the former than that of the latter. One sign of this is that one readily speaks of an "intended" but not of a "voluntary" outcome.

Interpreting the symbol "I" as "intentional" in the case of an act and "intended" in the case of an outcome is unlikely to cause difficulty. The same symbol has also been used for "indifference" for mnemonic reasons and with the expectation that the one-place predicates, Ia and Io_a, will readily be distinguished from the binary relation, oIo'.

2. Anyone who supposes that the task of distinguishing between intentional and nonintentional acts by means of secondary criteria is simple and straightforward will quickly be disabused of this notion if he reads two monographs on attempts to do just this, namely, Turner and Solomon (1962) on human escape and avoidance learning, and Goodrich (1966) on human eyeblink conditioning.

3. In any application of the formulas of this chapter, it goes without saying that all of the terms refer to the same individual organism. Whether *temporal* restrictions other than those inherent in the relation of empirical dependence and the act-outcome relation must be imposed is less obvious. An act may take place at a time much later than that at which the intention to perform it is thought to have been formed. If one visits a foreign city that one had "decided" years before to visit, it may be that the required preference and expectancies were present both at the time the "decision" was made and at the later time when the act, or complex of acts, was performed. The original intention or decision in such cases usually—perhaps always—has a contingent character; one seems to decide to visit Florence when one has time and money or, more vaguely, when circumstances permit.

On a smaller time scale—so much smaller that it is open to question whether the same rules apply—it is commonplace in experiments on reaction time, vigilance, verbal learning, problem-solving, and many others to require a subject to perform a particular act whenever a particular situation arises. He might, for example, be instructed to press a key as rapidly as he can when a buzzer sounds; and the buzzer might be scheduled to sound at irregular intervals during the experimental session. The differential outcomes for pressing the key *vs.* failing to do so, or for pressing it within a sufficiently short time, may be explicit money payoffs or may be the unstated approval or disapproval of the experimenter or of the subject himself. If the buzzer sounds and the subject presses the key, it is unlikely that a full-blown process of choice occurs in each instance; yet, rather than regarding the behavior as nonintentional, one is prone to suppose that it depended upon a process that was initiated when the instructions were given and that merely awaited the occurrence of the contingent situation to be completed. The term "set" is often applied to such preparatory processes.

These processes, whatever else may be said of them, appear to establish an interlocked triad involving the subject's preference for one of the differential outcomes over the other and act-outcome expectancies concerning the outcomes to be achieved, given the sounding of the buzzer, if he presses or does not press the key. The preference and expectancies may be thought of as existing in a "latent" form insofar as they do not affect the subject's behavior until the buzzer sounds. One meaning of *set* may then be *latent interlocked triad*.

It is possible for such a latent triad to give evidence of its existence when it is no longer appropriate—for example, in such a way as to produce a "wrong" response to the buzzer when the instructions have been changed to, "Now, do not press the key when the buzzer sounds." Under these conditions, presumably the expectancies have been changed and, indeed, are incompatible with those established by the original instructions. Such considerations suggest that forming an intention to perform an act when the opportunity arises at a later time is, in effect, to give over the control of the act to situational conditions; and this may well be the first step in the divorcement of the act from its dependency upon an interlocked triad and in its thus becoming automatized. The issues require more conceptual analysis and experimental work than they have received. Birenbaum's (1930) study of the forgetting of intentions made an interesting start that to the writer's knowledge has not been followed up.

4. The definition of a chosen act (6.7) specifies neither the rejected act nor the differential outcomes of the relevant triad; nor does the definition of the chosen outcome of an act (6.8) specify the rejected act or the nonchosen outcome. This reflects what can be meant by saying that different goals may be intended (on different occasions) by the same act or that the same goal may be intended (on different occasions) by different acts, and it suggests a nonmetaphysical sense in which organisms may be thought of as being free to choose among goals for an act or among acts for a goal. The amount of such freedom is the greater, the larger the organism's repertoire of intentional acts and the richer the environment's possibilities of outcomes of particular acts and the organism's acquaintance with these relations. Stone walls and iron bars may not, in some poetic sense, make prisons and cages, but they do prevent the enclosed person from doing things he would like to do and from realizing outcomes he would like to achieve; so, also, do loss of limbs, blindness, poverty, biases, and ignorance.

5. This can hardly be said of Anscombe's (1966) minute and interesting analysis of "intention." Her views are those of a philosopher rather than an experimental psychologist.

7

Diagnostic Rules of
Intentional Behavior

One reason for the use of the illustration from Miss Compton-Burnett's novel in the previous chapters is that it strikingly embodies one of the "diagnostic rules" that can now be discussed. It will be recalled that in this illustration, which enters now for the last time, the reader is given facts that may be interpreted in SAO language as follows: (1) the children intentionally abstained from warning their father of the danger to his life; (2) the occurrence of this act depended upon their expecting this act, rather than that of warning him, to result in his death; and (3) it also depended upon their expecting that warning him, rather than refraining from doing so, would result in his continued existence. When these facts became known to the father himself, he immediately concluded something that was not stated among them and that cannot be inferred from any one of them taken separately, namely, (4) that the children desired his death.

The effectiveness of this episode undoubtedly resides in the fact that the father, and the reader as well, find themselves in the position, not simply of being informed that the children have this desire, but of being compelled to *infer* the desire from other facts that taken singly are quite neutral. Fact (1)—abstaining from giving warning—would have been quite innocent if, for example, the children had known (or even had believed contrary to fact) that their father had already been warned. If in addition to this they had had reason to expect him to react negativistically to a warning from them, their act would appear in an even generous light. As to Fact (2), no blame attaches to the children merely from their expecting his death to result from their refraining from warning, rather than warning him. This represents no more than a correct appraisal of objective circumstances for which the children were in no way responsible. The same is true of Fact (3)—the children were not responsible for the likelihood that warning, rather than refraining from doing so, would result in his continued existence, nor for their appreciation of this. Furthermore, if they had actually given warning, these same expectancies would have been put to a praiseworthy use. Neither the act itself nor the children's expectancies are shocking; it is the fact that this particular act was determined by these two particular expectancies that transforms one's perception of the children from that of childish innocence to attribution of attempted patricide. The conclusion forces itself upon us that the act was also determined by a desire for their father's death and that this outcome was not only the expected, but also the preferred and intended, outcome of what they did.

RULES I, II, AND III

Rule I

The above conclusion does not follow from the definitions and assumptions of the previous chapters, but involves the implicit use of a principle of diagnosis. Abstracting from the particulars of the illustration, the rule says that: if an act is intentional and if its occurrence depends upon a pair of complementary act-outcome expectancies in which it figures as one of the alternative acts, then it also depends upon a preference for its expected outcome over the expected outcome of the alternative act. This will be called "Diagnostic Rule I," and can be stated formally as follows:

$$\{Ia \wedge [a * (aa'Eo \wedge a'aEo')]\} \rightarrow (a * oPo'). \qquad (7.1)$$

If Rule I holds, and if the act is chosen, it follows from the definition of a chosen act (6.7) and the first assumption concerning empirical dependence (6.1) that the preference exists. That is:

$$\{Ca \wedge [a * (aa'Eo \wedge a'aEo')]\} \rightarrow oPo'. \qquad (7.2)$$

Rule I is not restricted to cases as dramatic as Miss Compton-Burnett's. With a little alteration, each of the illustrations at the beginning of Chapter 6 exemplifies it. Considering Illustration 1, suppose (1) a child chooses to open a blue box, and this act is known to depend (2) upon the child's expecting that he will get a toy by doing this, rather than by opening a yellow box, and (3) upon his expecting that he will get a trinket if he opens the yellow box rather than the blue one. Then, (4) according to Rule I, the child must prefer getting a toy to getting a trinket. Illustrations 2 and 3 can readily be treated in the same way.

Rule II

Diagnostic Rule II is suggested by Rule I and considerations of symmetry. For variety, consider Illustration 2 of Chapter 6, altered to fit the present question. According to Rule II, if a subject in a signal-detection experiment (1) chooses to say "yes," and if this act depends (2) upon his preference for winning 5¢ over losing 5¢ and (3) upon his expecting that he will win 5¢ if he says "yes" rather than "no," then (4) he must also expect that he will lose 5¢ if he says "no" rather than "yes." In general, if an act is intentional and if it depends upon a preference and upon an act-outcome expectancy whose expected outcome is the preferred outcome, then it also depends upon a complementary expectancy, the expected outcome of which is the dispreferred outcome. In symbols, Rule II is:

$$\{Ia \wedge [a * (oPo' \wedge aa'Eo)]\} \rightarrow (a * a'aEo'). \tag{7.3}$$

If the act is chosen, it can be concluded that the second expectancy actually exists; the argument is the same as that for (7.2). Thus:

$$\{Ca \wedge [a * (oPo' \wedge aa'Eo)]\} \rightarrow a'aEo'. \tag{7.4}$$

Rule III

Diagnostic Rule III is parallel to the other two. In Illustration 3 of Chapter 6, if a dog (1) chooses to jump a hurdle from one side of a box to the other, and if this act depends (2) upon its preferring ω to shock and (3) upon its expecting to receive shock if it refrains from jumping rather than if it jumps, then (4) it must also expect to receive ω by jumping rather than by refraining from jumping. In general, if an act is intentional and depends upon a preference and upon an act-outcome expectancy whose expected outcome is the dispreferred outcome, then it also depends upon a complementary expectancy, the expected outcome of which is the preferred outcome. In symbols, Rule III is:

$$\{Ia \wedge [a * (oPo' \wedge a'aEo')]\} \rightarrow (a * aa'Eo). \tag{7.5}$$

If the act is chosen, it can be concluded that the second expectancy exists, by the argument for (7.2). Thus:

$$\{Ca \wedge [\text{a} * (oPo' \wedge a'aEo')]\} \rightarrow aa'Eo. \tag{7.6}$$

These diagnostic rules can be condensed into the following statements: *if an act is intentional and depends upon two members of an interlocked triad, then it also depends upon the third member of the triad. If, in addition, one of these rules holds and the act occurs (i.e., is chosen), then the third member of the triad exists.*

Rules I, II, and III are taken to be basic principles of a cognitive psychology. That they do not follow from the definition of intentional acts was asserted above and is demonstrated in Note 1 of this chapter. Nor can they be regarded as induced from experimental results; the required experiments do not exist. Rather, their formal status is that of empirical postulates, the credibility of which depends upon the fruitfulness of their application and the absence of persuasive counterexamples.

Although Note 1 shows that the rules do not require the use of secondary criteria of intentional acts, applications of the rules would be greatly facilitated by development of such criteria. It was remarked in Chapter 6 that, although such criteria are not very well established, this has not prevented experimenters and theorists from distinguishing between intentional and nonintentional acts on the basis of the form of the acts, their temporal course, their amplitudes, their latencies, and the relation of these to other variables. In the Compton-Burnett illustration, the intentionality of the children's act is judged from knowledge of the children's alertness and intelligence, from the deliberateness of the act as it was described, and from its obviously not falling into any of the main classes of nonintentional acts. Such judgments of individual events will always, of course, carry risks that a laboratory experimenter can reduce or eliminate. Of course, if we were wrong in regarding the act as intentional or as having depended upon the particular expectancies ascribed to it, our inference concerning the children's motivation would be invalid.

RULES I-a, II-a, AND III-a

If knowledge that an intentional act depends upon two members of an interlocked triad permits us to infer that it also depends upon the third member, as claimed by Rules I, II, and III, the question arises whether knowledge that an intentional act depends upon one member of a triad is sufficient for asserting that it depends upon the other two. Rules I-a, II-a, and III-a make this stronger claim. They are offered with some hesitation, partly because of their strength and partly because a significant exception to one of them, Rule I-a, is known and must be excluded on an *ad hoc* basis. Nevertheless, they lead to such plausible and useful results that it seems worthwhile to put them forward; more than this, Rule I-a is needed for the interpretation of the standard discrimination-preference experiment, as will be seen below. If the rules are found wanting, it may be that the objections themselves will throw further light on the nature of intentional behavior.

Rule I-a

Suppose we know that a child's intentionally opening a blue box depends (1) upon its preferring a toy to a trinket. Then, according to Rule I-a, if the child's preference is not a discriminandum for the occurrence of the act (a condition to be discussed below), we can conclude that this act also depends (2) upon the child's expecting to get a toy by performing this act rather than some unspecified alternative act and (3) upon its expecting to get a trinket if it performs this alternative act rather than opening the blue box. In general, if an act is intentional and depends upon a particular preference, and the preference is not a discriminandum for the act, then the act also depends upon a pair of complementary act-outcome expectancies interlocked with this act, with some unspecified alternative act, and with the differential outcomes specified by the preference. Formally, Rule I-a may be stated: given that oPo' is not a discriminandum for the occurrence of a,

$$[Ia \land (a * oPo')] \to [a * (\exists a') (aa'Eo \land a'aEo')]. \qquad (7.7)$$

If the act is chosen, and therefore occurs, this gives:

$$[Ca \land (a * oPo')] \to (\exists a') (aa'Eo \land a'aEo'). \qquad (7.8)$$

Rule II-a

If we know that a subject's intentionally saying "yes" in a signal-detection experiment depended upon (1) his expecting to win 5¢ by this act rather than by saying "no," Rule II-a states that we can conclude that his act depended (2) upon a preference for winning 5¢ over some unspecified differential outcome and (3) upon an expectancy that saying "no" rather than "yes" would lead to this same unspecified outcome. In general, if an act is intentional and depends upon the expectancy that it, rather than a specified alternative act, will lead to a particular outcome, then it also depends upon a preference for this outcome over some unspecified outcome and upon a complementary expectancy of which the dispreferred outcome is the expected outcome. Formally, Rule II-a may be stated:

$$[Ia \wedge (a * aa'Eo)] \rightarrow [a * (\exists o') (oPo' \wedge a'aEo')]. \tag{7.9}$$

If Act a occurs, then:

$$[Ca \wedge (a * aa'Eo)] \rightarrow (\exists o') (oPo' \wedge a'aEo'). \tag{7.10}$$

Rule III-a

Given that a dog's jumping intentionally from one side of a box to the other depends (1) upon its expecting that refraining from jumping, rather than jumping, will result in its receiving a shock, Rule III-a says that we can conclude that the jumping also depends (2) upon its preferring some unspecified differential outcome to shock and (3) upon its expecting that it will receive this unspecified outcome if it jumps rather than refrains from jumping. In general, if an act is intentional and depends upon the expectancy that a specified alternative act, rather than it, will lead to a particular outcome, then it also depends upon a preference for some unspecified outcome over this outcome and upon the complementary expectancy of which this unspecified outcome is the expected outcome. Formally, Rule III-a may be stated:

$$[Ia \wedge (a * a'aEo')] \rightarrow [a * (\exists o) (oPo' \wedge aa'Eo)]. \tag{7.11}$$

If Act a occurs, then:

$$[Ca \wedge (a * a'aEo')] \rightarrow (\exists o) (oPo' \wedge aa'Eo). \tag{7.12}$$

The Condition Upon Rule I-a

Rule I-a permits us to infer that an intentional act depends upon a certain pair of complementary act-outcome expectancies if we know that it depends upon a preference, subject to the condition that this preference is not a discriminandum for the act's occurrence. The need for this condition arises from the fact that if an organism can discriminate between two preference states (a problem to be discussed in Chapter 9), then in displaying such a discrimination it will use these states as discriminanda and will perform intentional acts that depend upon these discriminanda, just as in Table 3.5 the jumping behavior of Lashley's rats depended upon the discriminanda of pairs of circles of different diameters. We would then observe intentional acts the occurrence of which depended upon the presence of particular preferences, and Rule I-a, without the condition upon it, would imply that these acts were also determined by complementary expectancies interlocked with the preferences (with the alternative acts unspecified). But these expectancies need not exist; and if they did not, Rule I-a, minus the condition, would be contradicted.

As a further example, suppose that a human subject is able to discriminate between his own preference states of desiring food ($fP\omega$) and being averse to food (ωPf). If on a given occasion he reports correctly that he desires food, the act of reporting is presumably intentional and dependent upon $fP\omega$. But there are many circumstances under which the person would have no reason to expect that making this report, rather than performing some alternative act, would lead to *food*, nor that the alternative act, whatever it might be, would be more likely than the report to lead to ω. Yet Rule I-a, in the absence of the restriction put upon it, would imply that the reporting act was dependent upon just such expectancies. This kind of situation is discussed in detail in Chapter 9.

Rule I-a and the Standard
Discrimination-Preference Experiment

In earlier chapters, organisms' displays of discriminations, preferences, and expectancies in the standard discrimination-preference experiment (Table 3.7) and the standard act-outcome expectancy experiment (Table 5.2) have been used as prototypical of intentional behavior. It can be seen, however, that although the acts performed in a successful preference experiment depend upon the preference of which they are the evidence, and the acts in a successful expectancy experiment likewise depend upon the expectancies of which they are the evidence, further grounds must be provided for identifying the expectancies that are interlocked with the displayed preference in the first case and the preference that is interlocked with the displayed expectancies in the second case. The diagnostic rules provide these grounds.

Consider first the standard preference experiment as illustrated by Table 3.1. Moos's choices of acts were taken to show that he preferred food tokens to worthless tokens. Thus, in Condition 1, we may say that his opening the left panel depended upon his having this preference. If this behavior was intentional, we have, using the notation of the table, Ia_1 and $a_1 * o_1 P o_2$. Since the preference is presumed to have held under all conditions of the experiment, it was not a discriminandum for the occurrence of the acts and we may apply Rule I-a. Taking a_2 (opening the right panel) as the alternative act defined by the procedure, we have $a_1 * (a_1 a_2 E o_1 \wedge a_2 a_1 E o_2)$; and since a_1 was actually chosen in Condition 1, (7.8) implies that the two expectancies existed, $i.e.$, that $a_1 a_2 E o_1$ and $a_2 a_1 E o_2$. In the same way, it can be concluded that, in Condition 2, $a_2 * (a_2 a_1 E o_1 \wedge a_1 a_2 E o_2)$ and that these two expectancies existed in that condition, $i.e.$, that $a_2 a_1 E o_1$ and $a_1 a_2 E o_2$. Obviously, Conditions 1' and 2' can be dealt with similarly, the pairs of expectancies for Condition 1' being identical with those for Condition 2, and those for Condition 2' being identical with those of Condition 1.

According to this treatment of the discrimination-preference experiment, an organism is able to display discrimination because the two members of a pair of discriminanda arouse different expectancies. Thus, in Condition 1, d_1 (red on the left, green on the right) aroused $a_1 a_2 E o_1$ and $a_2 a_1 E o_2$, whereas in the concurrent Condition 2, d_2 (red on the right, green on the left) aroused $a_2 a_1 E o_1$ and $a_1 a_2 E o_2$. The reversal (Conditions 1' and 2') had the power of causing the expected o's to be interchanged between the discriminanda. That the discriminanda had the power to arouse particular act-outcome expectancies was, of course, a result of learning; Moos had to develop the expectancies and attach them differentially to the discriminanda by virtue of the relations that actually existed in the procedure among discriminanda, acts, and outcomes. With a human subject, a similar result might be obtained by instructing the subject about these relations verbally.

To apply Rule I-a to the standard discrimination-preference experiment, it was necessary to assume that the acts performed in that experiment were intentional. Although direct tests of this assumption are possible in principle, they would, of course, be arduous in practice. It would be much easier to test the adequacy of the rule itself, including the assumption, by determining independently whether the expectancies derived from applying the rule actually existed. The writer's view is that the arrangements of the standard discrimination-preference experiment exclude the possibility that the results are attributable to certain classes of nonintentional acts, such as reflexes, Pavlovian conditioned responses, and at least the simpler forms of "instinctive" acts as described, say, by ethologists. The principal danger seems to be that, if the experiment is carried on long enough, some degree of automatization might occur.

In the standard act-outcome expectancy experiment, as illustrated by Table 5.1, the organism's acts are shown by the experiment to depend upon the preference that is present in each condition and upon the act-outcome expectancies for which the results constitute the evidence. For example, we can conclude by virtue of the results of the experiment as a whole that (using the notation of the table), in Condition 1, $a_1 * (fPw \wedge a_1 a_2 Ef \wedge a_2 a_1 Ew)$. The three states upon which a_1 depended in this condition are an interlocked triad, and therefore a_1 was intentional; furthermore, since a_1 was chosen, the three states existed. This does not require the use of the diagnostic rules, but it does require the ability to identify the preference fPw in an appropriate preference experiment; and the interpretation of such an experiment has just been seen to involve the use of Rule I-a.

ILLUSTRATIVE APPLICATIONS OF THE RULES

1. Useful negative, as well as positive, diagnoses can be made by means of the rules. Imagine, for example, that Person A intentionally points a gun at Person B and pulls the trigger, with the result that B is shot and falls dead. Imagine, further, that there is acceptable evidence that A believed the gun to be empty, so that he did not expect that any act he chose to perform would cause it to fire and kill B. (The reader can readily devise any number of detective-story scenarios to fit the case.) Putting a_1 for this act, a' for an unspecified alternative act, and o_1 for the complex outcome of the gun firing and shooting B dead, we have $\sim(\exists a')a_1 a'Eo_1$. Then we can conclude that *A's act did not depend upon his desiring the outcome, o_1.*

This conclusion is reached as follows. If A's chosen act depended upon his desiring Outcome o_1, we could write, $Ca_1 \wedge (a * o_1 Pw)$. Putting this into (7.8) would lead to the inference that $(\exists a')a_1 a'Eo_1$. Since this contradicts the hypothesis, the act did not depend upon this desire.

2. It is interesting that, although the argument in the illustration just above showed that A's act did not depend upon his desiring the outcome that actually happened, it did *not* show that A was innocent of the desire itself. He may, indeed, have been very happy with the outcome even though he did not intend it. According to (6.2), the coincidence of the

desire and the act does not show that the act depended upon the desire. What preference the act did depend upon (for example, a desire to frighten or to anger B, or to ward off an attack from B, or the like) is left open by the facts as given.

3. The importance of precise identification of the elements in any preference or expectancy that is employed in the rules for diagnostic purposes may be indicated by further treatment of the same illustration. Imagine that A did not think the gun was loaded, but did expect that pointing the gun at B and pulling the trigger, rather than refraining from doing so, would cause B to die of fright. If A then performed this act intentionally and it depended upon this expectancy, Rule II-a indicates that A preferred B's death by fright to whatever was the expected outcome of refraining from the act. In this case, when the gun fired, A achieved part of his intended outcome, namely, B's death, but by means other than he had contemplated.

4. An intentional act may have consequences other than those that were intended. This creates problems for ethics, the law, and even esthetics (in view, for example, of action-painting and aleatory music), as well as for psychology, especially when the actor expects his act to have such unintended consequences. For example, a person may be more likely to do serious bodily harm to some other person if he chooses to drive an automobile than if he abstains from driving and may know that this is so; if he does know or believe this, then such an outcome must be regarded as an expected outcome of his act, although it will be recalled that this does not imply that the strength of the expectancy is great. Are we then forced by Rule II-a to suppose that his choosing to drive implies a preference for doing someone bodily harm over some other outcome, such as not harming anyone? Our answer is that no such conclusion follows from the rule unless the act of driving *depends* upon the expectancy, which presumably is usually not the case. If we could experimentally eliminate the expectancy and find that the person was no less likely to drive without it than with it, he would be absolved from the suspicion of a desire to hurt someone and, at the same time, the outcome of harming someone would be shown not to be an intended outcome of his driving.

Even cursory reading in jurisprudence shows that the legal conceptions of an intentional act differ in various ways from that defined by (6.5). The different purposes served by such a concept in the law and in psychology, aside from other considerations, would operate against identity of conception, desirable as it might be for distinct concepts to have distinct names. With respect to the present problem, that of expected but unintended outcomes of intentional acts, it is interesting to observe that Bentham (1948, p. 84; originally 1789) distinguished between "direct" and "oblique" consequences of an intentional act, the former being those the prospect of producing which was "one of the links in the chain of causes by which the person was determined to do the act," whereas the latter were those in the case of which "although the consequence was in contemplation, and appeared likely to ensue in case of the act's being performed, yet the prospect of producing such consequences did not constitute a link in the aforesaid chain." Our distinction, although made in ignorance of Bentham's views, appears to agree closely with them on this point. Hart, to whom we are indebted for the quotations from Bentham, shows that the law sometimes treats what we would call expected but unintended outcomes of acts as if they were intended (1968, pp. 118-122).

Although one may be skeptical of the psychoanalytic view that the point of making omelets is the unholy pleasure of breaking eggs, it would be a mistake to reject the notion altogether. One is surely tempted to disavow, to a critic or to oneself, responsibility for an outcome that can readily be seen as an undesired and unintended side-effect of an act that had also an obviously acceptable consequence.

SUMMARY

Rules are offered that permit one to infer that an intentional act depends upon all three members of an interlocked triad if it is known to depend upon two members of such a triad (Rules I, II, and III) or even if it is only known to depend upon one member (Rules I-a, II-a, and III-a). In the latter case, the rules always leave one of the elements (an alternative act or differential outcome) unspecified. The rules do not derive from the definition of an intentional act, but are taken to have the formal status of empirical postulates. Illustrative applications of the rules are given, and the relation of one of them (Rule I-a) to the standard discrimination-preference experiment and the standard act-outcome expectancy experiment is discussed.

NOTES AND COMMENTS

1. That Rules I, II, and III do not follow from the definition of an intentional act can be seen as follows. Suppose that the occurrence of Act a_1 depends upon the triad o_1Po_2, $a_1a_2Eo_1$, and $a_2a_1Eo_2$. Then, by definition, a_1 is intentional (6.5). Suppose that the occurrence of a_1

depends, in addition, upon two other expectancies, $a_1 a_2 Eo_3$ and $a_2 a_1 Eo_4$, but *not* upon the preference $o_3 Po_4$. This is compatible with the intentionality of a_1, since the definition requires that the act depend upon an interlocked triad but does not prevent its depending also upon other states. But this same state of affairs contradicts Rule I, which requires that the act shall depend upon $o_3 Po_4$ if it is intentional and depends upon $a_1 a_2 Eo_3$ and $a_2 a_1 Eo_4$. Since Rule I puts restrictions upon the determiners of an intentional act that the definition of an intentional act does not, the rule does not follow from the definition.

2. It might be thought that the conclusion of (7.4) could be derived from its antecedent together with (5.5), but this is not so. The antecedent of (7.4),

$$Ca \wedge [\mathbf{a} * (oPo' \wedge aa'Eo)],$$

can be expanded by (6.4) and (6.7) to:

$$Ia \wedge \mathbf{a} \wedge (\mathbf{a} * oPo') \wedge (\mathbf{a} * aa'Eo).$$

Dropping the first three terms of this expression, by the logical rule of simplification, and using (6.1), we have:

$$\mathbf{a} \to aa'Eo.$$

By *modus ponens*, this, together with **a** (from the hypothesis), gives:

$$aa'Eo.$$

Hence, by (5.5):

$$(\exists o')a'aEo'.$$

Here, however, the Outcome o' remains unspecified, whereas in the conclusion of (7.4) it is specified as the dispreferred outcome in oPo'. Thus, Rule II has a stronger conclusion than can be reached by conjunction of its antecedent and (5.5). The same can be said of the relation between Rule III (7.6) and (5.5).

3. It was said above (p. 93) that, when an organism displays a discrimination, the discriminanda arouse different act-outcome expectancies. It may be of interest to examine Terrace's "errorless discrimination learning" in the light of this conception.

Terrace (1963) trained pigeons to peck at a red key for food reward. He then intermixed with such trials occasions on which the key was a very faint green of short duration; gradually, over trials, the green became more intense and lasted longer until finally the red (S+) and green (S –) were of equal duration and of equal apparent intensity. In this way the pigeons were brought to a point at which they always pecked at the key when it was red and never when it was green without ever having made the "error" of pecking the key when it was green. A similar phenomenon has been demonstrated with children; see, *e.g.*, Gollin and Savoy (1968).

Is this "discrimination" in the strong sense in which the term is used here? Clearly, the procedure does not amount to a standard discrimination experiment; first, the experimenter provides no differential outcomes for pecking *vs.* not pecking at the green, and in any case such outcomes would be ineffective in the absence of pecking at green; and, second, no reversal procedure was run—had this been done, the subjects would have been forced into errors. On the face of it, we have evidence for differential response to a c.p.f. containing red *vs.* the same c.p.f. containing green, but not for discrimination between red and green.

We can ask, however, whether the animals were in fact discriminating between red and green, even though the procedure did not permit them to give full evidence of it. Without denying that pigeons are quite capable of making this easy discrimination, there are grounds for answering this question in the negative. Rather, what Terrace's procedure seems to have achieved was to make the pigeons treat the c.p.f. with green in it no differently than the c.p.f. alone, as if they were "paying no attention" to the green.

If we suppose that the pecking behavior under these conditions was intentional, it can be claimed that the original training to red resulted in their discriminating between the c.p.f. alone and the c.p.f. with red, *i.e.*, between δ and red, which is what we would call "detection" of red. (The fact that it is easy does not remove it from the realm of detection.) By an SAO interpretation of such behavior, red aroused the act-outcome expectancies that pecking rather than refraining from pecking would lead to food and that refraining from pecking, rather than pecking, would lead to ω, whereas δ aroused the act-outcome expectancies that refraining from pecking rather than pecking would lead to ω and that pecking would lead to unrequited effort, frustration, or the like. Green was never pecked at; consequently, no differential outcomes of pecking and of not pecking at green were experienced, so that the same act-outcome expectancies were aroused by the c.p.f. plus green as by the c.p.f. alone (δ). Hence, the pigeons continued to exhibit detection of red during the intermixture of red and green trials. Of course, if the behavior was nonintentional, which is by no means unlikely in the case of pecking behavior in pigeons, even the pecking to red was not an exhibition of discrimination, but only of differential response. That pecking behavior in pigeons is hard to classify along conventional lines has been shown by Williams and Williams (1969), among others.

Terrace recognized, and indeed made much of, the differences (for example, flat gradients of stimulus generalization to S−) between the behavior following "errorless discrimination learning" and that produced by more usual procedures. These differences led him to say (Terrace, 1966, p. 1678) that ". . . after discrimination is learned without errors, S− appears to function as a neutral stimulus," a statement that appears to mean the same thing as our claim that the c.p.f. with green is treated no differently from the c.p.f. alone (δ). In the same paper he also said (p. 1680) that when the subject learns with errors, it ". . . learns to respond to S+ and not to respond to S−," whereas when the subject learns without errors, it ". . . learns to respond to S+ and not to its absence." As far as these statements go, they seem congruent with our interpretation of the former case as one of discrimination between red and green and the latter as one of detection of red.

With human subjects and the use of language, it should not be hard to produce errorless learning of a discrimination between, say, a red light and a green light, without gradual introduction of either light. One would need only to induce the appropriate act-outcome expectancies by telling the subject what would happen if he performed each of a pair of alternative acts in the presence of each of the lights. On further tests, such learning would probably have the properties ascribed by Terrace to learning *with* errors; for example, one would expect the subject to behave in stimulus-generalization tests much as he would have behaved if he had acquired the act-outcome expectancies without instructions and with whatever errors were entailed by his having to learn by trial what outcome resulted from what act in the presence of each of the lights. What is important is not whether errors are made, but what expectancies the subject forms in the particular procedure he is exposed to.

Nothing in these comments reduces the interest in Terrace's findings. One could not know in advance how effective his gradual procedures of introducing an "irrelevant" stimulus would be, and further study of the phenomena will no doubt advance knowledge and theory of "attention," if not of discrimination.

PART II

Some Problems, Applications, and
Extensions of the System

8

Review and Prospect

The preceding seven chapters have been devoted to the construction of a number of psychological concepts, including, among others, preference, indifference, preferred and dispreferred outcome, discrimination, act-outcome expectancy, expected outcome, desire, aversion, neutrality, intentional act, intended outcome, chosen act, and chosen outcome. Each of these concepts was defined by logical and empirical relations among the undefined or primitive concepts of situation, act, and outcome. Underlying all this were, of course, the unstated assumptions of experimental science.

IS PART I A THEORY?

A set of interrelated concepts is not a scientific theory; for this, empirical relations between these concepts and other, independently observable, variables are required. With certain exceptions, such relations have not been formally asserted, but many of them have been suggested or assumed in the illustrations. For example, it was supposed that rats deprived of food or water for some length of time would prefer food or water to the null differential outcome, ω; it was supposed that the desiredness of a food token for a chimpanzee was acquired through some sort of experience in which such tokens were exchangeable for food; and it was supposed that a human subject's expectancy that saying "yes" rather than "no" under certain conditions would gain him 5¢ could be acquired by his receiving appropriate instructions from an experimenter. These suppositions were not part of the argument that led to the construction of the set of concepts; they were embodied in illustrations that were intended to clarify and make plausible the argument, but the logic of the argument itself did not depend upon their factual correctness.

Some assertions have been made that do, however, have theoretical status. These include the assumption that preferences are transitive under certain restrictions; the assumption that act-outcome expectancies are transitive with regard to their acts, under similar restrictions; and all of the diagnostic principles stated in Chapter 7. These assertions have in common the fact that they are so general and so far removed from direct experimental tests that they might be regarded as pretheoretical empirical postulates rather than empirical rules or laws.

It may be concluded, then, that Part I contains elements of a psychological system together with some theory explicitly stated and a good deal more informally assumed in the illustrations. The words "system" and "theory" will be used freely in the remaining chapters as each seems appropriate to the context.

NATURE OF THE THEORY

The theory for which Part I attempts to lay the foundations is of the kind commonly called "cognitive," because it supposes that intentional behavior depends upon the organism's knowledge or cognitions of situations and outcomes. Such a theory may be thought of as neo-Tolmanian, in recognition of Edward C. Tolman, the most influential cognitive theorist of modern psychology. The particular system that is presented here may be called a situation-act-outcome, or SAO, psychology, since its concepts are constructed from these three primitive terms.

Although this point of view differs, and in some cases differs sharply, from other current views, the intention of this book is not polemical. After the largely futile search during the past forty or fifty years for crucial experiments to decide between cognitive and stimulus-response theories, it has become apparent that choices at this level of abstraction are to a considerable degree matters of scientific strategy and that the eventual results of such choices are more likely to be visible, not after decisive single tests, but at a date so much later than that of the choices that the intervening research and theoretical work may have altered the situation beyond recognition.

Nevertheless, as was just said, the present system is unlike certain other systems that are now guiding research and theorizing. Some of the differences will be mentioned here, but they will become clearer to the reader as particular problems are dealt with in later chapters.

Primitive Terms

The present system employs three primitive terms, situation, act, and outcome, whereas much, if not most, of contemporary experimental psychology employs only two, stimulus and response. Reinforcement might be thought of as a third primitive, but it is usually defined functionally by its relation to responses or stimulus-response connections. Although there is an obvious parallel between situation and stimulus, on the one hand, and act and response, on the other, the tendency of S–R theorists is toward reduction of stimuli to physical energies impinging upon receptors and reduction of responses to physiologically defined effector actions, whereas SAO theory analyzes situations and acts only as far as is necessary for the purpose immediately at hand and does not assume that they are eventually reducible to physics and physiology. At the same time, SAO theory at no point supposes that behavior violates physical or biological laws; it is not "vitalistic."

The most elementary constructions of S–R theory are S–R connections; those of SAO theory are preferences, discriminations, and act-outcome expectancies, all of which involve the concept of outcome as a primitive. The simplest behavior dealt with by S–R theory is the running off of an S–R connection, as in simple reflexes or elementary habits. SAO theory recognizes such behavior, but it does not treat intentional behavior as reducible to it.

Learning

The major effort of S–R theory has been spent upon problems of learning, and S–R theories are distinguished one from another primarily by their particular hypotheses concerning this process. This may be a historical accident, but it has set the tone of theoretical construction and debate in psychology, at least in the United States, for most of this century. The present system, on the other hand, happened to develop from consideration of motivational problems, and it is to such problems that its applications in this book are mainly addressed.

Although this, too, may be an accident of history, Tolman's view of learning as the process of acquisition and modification of expectancies put him into opposition with S–R theories of the type of Thorndike's and Hull's in which learning was conceived of as the strengthening of S–R connections by "effect," i.e., the occurrence of satisfiers or "reinforcements." It is clear today that two distinct problems are entangled in such an opposition. One of these is the problem of the locus of learning, which for Tolman was in expectancies and for Hull and Thorndike was in S—R connections. The other is the problem of the fundamental laws of learning, and whether or not, for example, these must include reference to Thorndikian satisfiers or Hullian or Skinnerian reinforcers.

In the SAO treatment of intentional behavior, learning in the form of acquisition and modification of expectancies plays a central role. Indeed, an organism must exhibit such learning to meet the criteria of the standard experiments for preference, discrimination, and act-outcome expectancy. It will not be supposed that positive or negative preference-value of outcomes is required for this process, and it will be found possible to discuss a wide range of problems without suffering from the fact that the concept of reinforcement in a Hullian or Skinnerian sense will be completely absent. It can nevertheless be left for detailed study of learning to determine as a question of law, rather than hypothesis, what effects, if any, the values of outcomes may have upon changes in expectancies.

Two further suppositions will be made. First, it will be supposed that Pavlovian conditioning of certain acts, which then may properly be called responses, takes place; and this will lead to a two-factor account of special cases of "emotional" motivation in Chapter 12. Second, it will be supposed that a process of automatization of situation-act relations occurs; this means that an act that is intentional at one point in its history becomes at a later point less dependent upon, or even wholly independent of, current expectancies and preferences. There is little difference, if any, between such situation-act relations and S—R connections, aside from the systems in which they are embedded, but in SAO theory they constitute a special case, rather than the whole subject matter of the system.

States and Processes

Preferences and expectancies are dispositional states of the organism, and changes in such states, such as "learning," are processes. Psychology attempts to relate such states and processes to prior and concomitant variables, on the one hand, and to acts, on the other. In a logical sense, then, they are intervening variables. The view taken here is, however, that they are observable objects, and no more hypothetical than the inflammability of a dry match or the noninflammability of a wet match. Furthermore, such states and processes are not only observable, but have been observed. As observed facts, their significance for psychology can be debated but their existence cannot be doubted without questioning the numerous experiments whose results can be put into the standard forms described in Chapters 3 and 5.

The existence of preferences, expectancies, and other states and processes is known by way of behavior; and it must be supposed that an organism that is in a particular state at a particular time is organically different from what it would be were it not in that state. This is the fundamental postulate of physiological psychology. It is important, however, to keep in mind the fact that this postulate does not imply a relation of identity between psychological and physiological states. The two are defined in different terms: psychological states by relations among situations, acts, and outcomes, and physiological states by terms from anatomy, chemistry, and physics. The closest possible relation between the two would be a one-to-one existence relation, that is, a strong empirical law to the effect that a given psychological state exists when and only when a given independently defined physiological state exists. This makes a "reduction" of psychology to physiology impossible by definition, but it puts no limit upon the usefulness and significance of physiological psychology. Psychology can only benefit by every advance toward strong psychophysiological laws.

Consciousness

As the reader has seen, it has not been necessary to introduce the notion of "consciousness" in defining intentional acts, intended outcomes, and the psychological states prior to these in the present system. The notion itself is extraordinarily vague; and Miller (1942) claims to have found as many as sixteen distinct meanings of its opposite, "unconsciousness."

To say that an organism is conscious of something becomes meaningful in an SAO system if appropriate behavioral criteria can be found to assess the factual correctness of such a statement. The problem hardly arises seriously as long as we are dealing with organisms that display differential responses and biases but not discriminations and act-outcome expectancies, of which the blowfly (Dethier, 1964, 1966) is probably an example. When the latter states appear, some might wish to claim that the organism was conscious of the discriminanda and outcomes that are the objects of these states, which we have already loosely described above as cognitive. The demand would no doubt be still stronger if the organism were able to meet criteria of "perception" of objects; such criteria have not been offered here, but would presumably be stronger than those of discrimination. If, finally, the organism were able to perceive its own psychological states, as human beings can no doubt sometimes do, then, if ever, it would surely be said to be "conscious" of them.

A reader who follows this line of thought with any degree of sympathy may be led, like the writer, to wonder whether the concept of consciousness has any nonredundant meaning at all. If it does, it would seem to have the same criteria as those of perception but to be more general, in that it would refer to cognitions of all kinds of objects whatsoever, including psychological states themselves, rather than being restricted, as perception often is, to cognitions of objects that are non-psychological.

At any rate, SAO theory supposes that to perceive something and to be conscious that one perceives it, or to desire something and to be conscious that one desires it, are two different things, and that the former member of each of these pairs by no means implies the latter. In the writer's view, consciousness in this sense is much less prevalent and accurate than it is often taken to be. Freud has perhaps done psychology a disservice, not by insisting upon the significance of unconscious processes (in his special meaning of this term), but by unintentionally giving more significance than it deserves to the difference between states of which the person is conscious and those of which he is not.

TOPICS OF PART II

The concepts developed in Part I will be applied in Part II, sometimes in extended forms, to a variety of psychological problems. Chapter 9 will discuss illustrative experiments that have been designed to determine whether an organism as far below the psychological capacities of human beings as the laboratory rat is able to discriminate its own motivational states, a question related to the discussion of "consciousness" in the immediately preceding paragraphs. Chapter 10 will deal with the parallel problem whether such an organism can exhibit preferences among its own motivational states or, in particular, whether it can be said that such states are desired or aversive. This question bears upon the significance of the familiar concept of "drive."

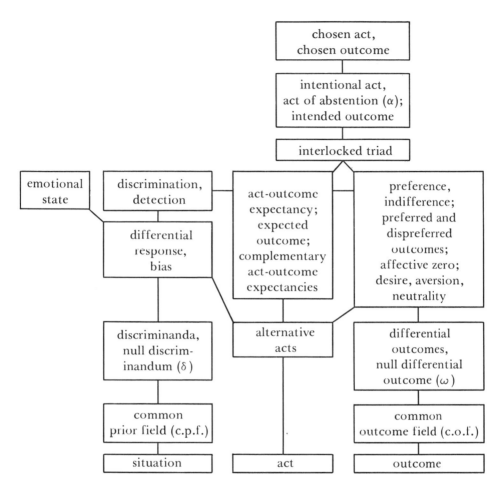

Fig. 8.1. Concepts employed in the SAO system of Part I

Connections between boxes at different levels indicate definition dependence of concepts at higher levels upon those at lower levels. Horizontal connections indicate relations among empirical criteria. (The concept of "emotional state" is discussed in Chapter 12.)

Chapter 11 will offer suggestions and speculations about motivational and cognitive aspects of intentional behavior. It will put forward criteria of general and specific "motives" and discuss the relation of general motives to "concepts," the problem of impossible outcomes, the analysis of complex intentional acts and intended outcomes, and the relation of SAO theory to decision theory, psychological hedonism, and what may be called the "flow of behavior." Finally, Chapter 12 will present views on the relation of intentional behavior to quantitative properties of acts, a matter that will turn out to be closely associated with the concept of "emotion."

SUMMARY

The set of interrelated concepts that has been developed in Part I is represented in full in Fig. 8.1. Because these concepts were defined by logical and empirical relations among the three basic concepts of situation, act, and outcome, the structure is called a situation-act-outcome, or SAO, system. The theory can be characterized as "cognitive" or neo-Tolmanian. Features that distinguish it from most other current theories are the concepts it employs, its avoidance of a Thorndikian "effect" or "reinforcement" hypothesis of instrumental learning, its relegation of the notion of "drive" to a subsidiary position, its provision of empirical criteria for each of the psychological states with which it is concerned, and its leaving open the question of the extent to which situations, acts, and outcomes are reducible to elements, physical or physiological, at lower levels of abstraction. The theory is not, however, vitalistic, and it welcomes advances in physiological psychology. Problems of "consciousness" are taken to be factual questions concerning organisms' cognitions.

9

Discrimination among States

Objects of discrimination are not limited to external physical objects like those that were used in the illustrations of Chapter 3. An organism's own psychological states, for example, vary from time to time and the question can be asked whether the organism can discriminate among them. Human beings are often deeply interested in their own psychological states and believe that they can identify many of them and can make fine distinctions among them. Thus, they speak of themselves as being hungry, thirsty, in love, tired, surprised, stupid, angry, frightened, bored, and the like, and are prepared to use any one of these states as the main heading for a discussion full of shadings and niceties.

The present chapter is limited to a narrow segment of this area of problems, and asks: how can we know whether a human being or other organism discriminates between two of his own psychological states? The strictly experimental literature on this matter is, to the writer's knowledge, largely restricted to studies concerned with rats' ability to discriminate between the states induced by food-deprivation (FD) and water-deprivation (WD). Highly specialized as this is, it provides examples of problems of method and interpretation that arise when one wishes to use an organism's own states as discriminanda for its behavior and of the application of SAO theory to these problems.

It is well known that work on an organism's ability to discriminate between its own states of "hunger" and "thirst" was initiated by Hull (1933). Because he thought of "drives" as general undirected energizers, he was led to the notion that each drive had a characteristic "drive stimulus" associated with it, which entered into the process of learning like other stimuli and accounted for the fact that behavior as it is learned becomes appropriate to the particular drive involved in the learning. Thus, a hungry animal can learn to perform acts that have led it to food, and a thirsty animal to perform acts that have led it to water, because the drive stimuli of hunger and thirst constitute important differentiating features of the whole stimulus situation in each case. It is natural, then, to ask whether such drive stimuli, like other stimuli, can serve as objects of discrimination. In SAO language, Hull was asking whether drive stimuli can function as discriminanda not merely for differential response but for discrimination in the strong sense. Hull's work led to a considerable amount of research, of which we shall give several examples.

The problem of determining whether an organism can discriminate between two of its own states is a special case of the problem of its discrimination between any pair of discriminanda. Clearly, the solution is to perform a standard discrimination experiment like those of Chapter 3, using the two states as discriminanda and choosing some convenient pair of differential outcomes between which the organism is known to have a preference. The special difficulties derive from the requirement that the experimenter be able to identify the two states and have them under experimental control. To find out whether a subject can discriminate between, say, the states of anger and fear, one would like to be able to turn each of these states on and off at will; but methods for doing this are not readily available. Similarly, to find out whether a subject can discriminate between its own states of preferring food to water and preferring water to food, it is necessary to test the subject sometimes in the one state and sometimes in the other in a random order over a series of trials. This is not altogether impracticable if the trials are spaced and if one relies upon FD and WD as inducers of these states and upon satiation procedures as reducers of them. The experimental work that will be described has relied upon such operations.

BESCH, MORRIS, AND LEVINE'S EXPERIMENT

An experiment by Besch, Morris, and Levine (1963, Group NC-A) is represented in Table 9.1. The discriminanda were whatever differential states are aroused by FD, WD, and satiation with food or water. Tentatively, for the purpose of the present discussion, we shall suppose that these states were a preference for food over water, *fPw*, and a preference for water over food, *wPf*. Rats were run in a T-maze. When they were under FD, a right turn led to a goalbox containing a familiar rat of the same sex and a left turn led to an empty box (which we take

Table 9.1
Discrimination between states resulting from FD and WD
(after Besch, Morris, and Levine,
1963, Group NC-A)

	Situations	
	Series I	
	d_1 : FD (fPw)	d_2 : WD (wPf)
a_1 : turning right	+ o_1 : social rat	− o_2 : ω
a_2 : turning left	− o_2 : ω	+ o_1 : social rat

Note: No reversal was run.

to be ω); when they were under WD, a right turn led to ω and a left turn to the familiar rat. On the basis of previous information, it was presumed that the rats preferred the "social rat" (s) to ω, *i.e.*, $sP\omega$. The rats' problem, as in any standard discrimination experiment, was to choose the act that led to the preferred outcome; here, the only available cues were presumed to be the differential states resulting from FD and WD.

As Table 9.1 indicates, the animals succeeded in solving this problem. On the assumption that the results of the reversal conditions of the standard experiment would have been positive, of which there seems to be no ground for serious doubt, we may conclude that the rats did indeed exhibit the required discrimination. Although Besch *et al.* did not present data for right and left turns separately, the fact that the rats attained an overall level of about 80% correct trials by the end of the experiment suggests that they were performing at a level better than that of chance under each of the two conditions.

Table 9.2
Discrimination between states resulting from
11½ and 47½ hr. FD
(Jenkins and Hanratty, 1949)

	Situations	
	Series I	
	d_1: 11½ hr. FD $(fP\omega)_1$	d_2: 47½ hr. FD $(fP\omega)_2$
a_1: turning right	+ o_1: food	− o_2: ω
a_2: turning left	− o_2: ω	+ o_1: food

Note: No reversal was run.

On the assumption that reversal conditions would have succeeded, the results not only demonstrate the discrimination that was at issue, but also the preference for the social rat over ω ($sP\omega$) that was initially assumed. If the rats had been indifferent between s and ω, the experiment would have failed.

JENKINS AND HANRATTY'S EXPERIMENT

Jenkins and Hanratty (1949) asked whether rats could discriminate between two different degrees of hunger, i.e., the states resulting from 11½ and 47½ hours of FD. In their procedure (Table 9.2) a right turn in a T-maze led to food and a left turn to an empty box (ω) under the shorter FD, whereas a right turn led to ω and a left turn to food under the longer FD. Positive results were obtained, as indicated in the table. No reversal procedure was run; but on the assumption that it would have been successful, the required discrimination was demonstrated.

The deprivation conditions may be presumed to have induced two intensities of desire for food; let us call the weaker intensity $(fP\omega)_1$ and the stronger $(fP\omega)_2$. Let us further suppose, for the moment, that it was these states that were discriminated. Then it can be seen that the differential outcomes of food and ω were both the actual outcomes of the choices and the objects of preference in the states that were employed as discriminanda. In the experiment of Besch et al., however, if the discriminated states are taken to be fPw and wPf, the differential outcomes of food and water that are related by these states are distinct from the differential outcomes of social rat and ω that were actually obtained by the choices. Thus, in the present experiment, the states $(fP\omega)_1$ and $(fP\omega)_2$ had two functions: first, as discriminanda, to arouse two different pairs of complementary expectancies; and secondly, to provide the motivating preferences for the choices. In the case of Besch et al., the first of these functions was performed by fPw and wPf as discriminanda, whereas the second, or motivating function, was performed by the preference for the social rat over ω, $sP\omega$.

The differences between the two experiments can be clarified by writing the formulas for the intentional acts performed by the subjects at late stages in training. For the experiment of Besch et al., we can write the formulas as follows, using r for turning right, l for turning left, and s for the social rat:

$$\text{under } d_1 \;[(fPw)]: \quad r * (sP\omega \wedge rlEs \wedge lrE\omega);$$

$$\text{under } d_2 \;[(wPf)]: \quad l * (sP\omega \wedge rlE\omega \wedge lrEs).$$

Note that the motivating preference, $sP\omega$, occurs in both conditions as the motivating preference in the interlocked triads and is distinct from the discriminanda, fPw and wPf, each of which occurs in only one of the conditions. For the experiment of Jenkins and Hanratty, the conditions are:

$$\text{under } d_1 \;[(fP\omega)_1]: \quad r * [(fP\omega)_1 \wedge rlEf \wedge lrE\omega)];$$

$$\text{under } d_2 \;[(fP\omega)_2]: \quad l * [(fP\omega)_2 \wedge rlE\omega \wedge lrEf)].$$

Here, the states $(fP\omega)_1$ and $(fP\omega)_2$ appear *twice* in each condition, once as a discriminandum and once as the motivating preference in the interlocked triad.

There appear to be no grounds in principle for preferring one of these two sorts of experiments to the other, although the psychological analysis of the experiment by Besch *et al.* has an esthetic advantage in clearly separating the functions of states as discriminanda and as motivators. Research might, of course, find that one type was superior to the other in efficiency.

PROBLEMS OF METHOD AND INTERPRETATION

Hull's Experiment

Hull's (1933) pioneering experiment had certain features that point up problems of interpretation when contrasted with later work. Rats were run in a rectangular maze (Fig. 9.1). The correct path required them either to turn right at a choice-point when they emerged from the startbox and follow the alley around the right half of the rectangle or to turn left from the startbox and follow the alley around the left half of the rectangle; in either case, they arrived at the same goalbox. The goalbox contained food when they were under FD and water when they were under WD. The incorrect path for a given condition had a barrier just ahead of the goalbox. If the rat chose this path and went to the barrier, it was permitted to retrace to the choice-point (but not to re-enter the startbox) and get to the goalbox along the other side of the maze; this is known as a "correction" procedure.

The conditions are outlined in Table 9.3. Considering Series I, it can be seen that, under FD, the rats obtained food by the direct path if they turned right; but if they turned left, they found the barrier (if they ran that far), retraced, and then obtained food. On the other hand, in the same Series, if the rats were under WD, they obtained water by the direct path if they turned left, but if they turned right, they had to retrace and thus obtain water by the indirect path. Series II reversed the relation of the initial turn to the outcomes.

We may tentatively assume for Hull's experiment, as we did for that of Besch *et al.*, that the discriminanda were the preference states *fPw* and *wPf*. (Hull supposed that they were differential drive stimuli for hunger and thirst.) What, however, were the motivating preferences for the choices? Hull's subjects did in fact learn to choose the "correct" paths more frequently than the "incorrect" paths, although only after many trials of practice. The states *fPw* and *wPf* could not, however,

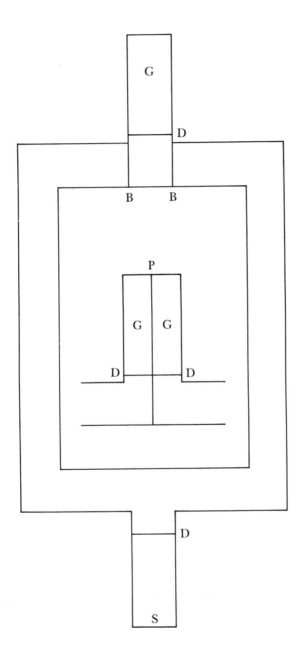

Fig. 9.1. Schematic diagram of maze used by Hull (1933). Inset:
Goalbox arrangements in maze used by Leeper (1935),
Experiment III-C. S: starting box; G: goalbox; D: door;
B: barrier; P: partition

Table 9.3
Discrimination between states resulting from FD and WD
(Hull, 1933)

	Conditions			
	Series I		Series II	
	d_1: FD (fPw)	d_2: WD (wPf)	d_1: FD (fPw)	d_2: WD (wPf)
a_1: turning right	+ o_1: food	− o_2: barrier, retracing, water	− o_2: barrier, retracing, food	+ o_1: water
a_2: turning left	− o_2: barrier, retracing, food	+ o_1: water	+ o_1: food	− o_2: barrier, retracing, water

Note: Series I and II were run on different subjects.

function as sufficient motivating preferences for correct choices, since the rats always obtained food under *fPw* and water under *wPf*, whether they turned right or left at the choice-point. It is clear that the results demonstrate a preference for the differential outcomes of *a direct path over an indirect path* to a preferred outcome. Whether this represents a preference for less work over more work, or an aversion to a state of "frustration" generated by finding a barrier, or something else that is differentially associated with the paths cannot be determined from the results of this experiment alone. It should be noted that this problem of identifying the preferences that motivated the subjects' choices is not crucial for the purpose of the experiment. Whatever these preferences may have been, the rats exhibited a discrimination between the consequences of FD and WD.

Table 9.4
Learning under states resulting from FD and WD
(Leeper, 1935)

		Conditions		
		Series I		Series II	
		d_1: FD (fPw)	d_2: WD (wPf)	d_1: FD (fPw)	d_2: WD (wPf)
a_1: turning right		+ o_1: food, eating	− o_1: food, retracing, water, drinking	− o_2: water, retracing, food, eating	+ o_2: water, drinking
a_2: turning left		− o_2: water, retracing, food, eating	+ o_2: water, drinking	+ o_1: food, eating	− o_1: food, retracing, water, drinking

Note: Series I and II were run on different subjects.

Leeper's Experiment

Consider now an experiment of Leeper (1935), which is often cited as a successful attempt to reduce the difficulty of this sort of problem and therefore to enable animals to exhibit the discrimination in fewer training trials than Hull's rats had required. We restrict the discussion to Leeper's Experiment III-C, the design of which is shown in Table 9.4. Leeper ran rats in a rectangular maze like Hull's, but (in the experiment under discussion) introduced a partition that divided the goalbox into right and left halves (see the inset in Fig. 9.1). In Series I, the right side always contained food and the left side water; in Series II the reverse was the case. A correction procedure was used. Considering Series I, if the rat was under FD, an initial right turn led to food, whereas a left turn led to water (the less preferred outcome), and food was obtained by retracing past the starting point, around the other side of the maze, and eventually to food; if the rat was under WD, a left turn led to water, whereas a right turn led to food (now the less preferred outcome), retracing, and eventually to water. Series II involved reversal of the relations between initial turns and differential outcomes. As the table indicates, the animals were able to solve the problem.

Putting aside Leeper's division of the goalbox as irrelevant for the present point, the outlines of Leeper's and Hull's experiments are very similar, as can be seen by comparing Tables 9.3 and 9.4. There is, nevertheless, one difference that is crucial for interpretation of the results (as Leeper perceived). If one looks at the outcomes of *incorrect* choices, one sees that Leeper's animals, if they went all the way to the goalbox, always found the dispreferred outcome there; but this was never true of Hull's animals, which met a barrier that prevented them from entering the goalbox or observing its contents on incorrect runs. Leeper's procedure constitutes an act-outcome expectancy experiment (Chapter 5), not a discrimination experiment (Chapter 3), and its results cannot tell us whether the rats were discriminating between the states resulting from FD and WD.

The point is that it was not *necessary* for Leeper's animals to make the desired discrimination in order to solve the problem they were faced with. The differential states, fPw and wPf, may have functioned only as motivating preferences for the choices, not as discriminanda. The animals had the opportunity to learn in Series I, for example, that food was obtained by turning right rather than left ($rlEf$) and that water was obtained by turning left rather than right ($lrEw$). Given these two expectancies, a choice of a right turn under FD and a left turn under WD would not require the preference states to be used as discriminanda. At an advanced stage in training, the animals in Condition 1 would know that food was always on the right and water always on the left, and the formulas would be:

under FD: $r * (fPw \wedge rlEf \wedge lrEw)$;

under WD: $l * (wPf \wedge rlEf \wedge lrEw)$.

Table 9.5
Discrimination between states resulting from FD and WD
(after Cheng, 1960)

	Conditions			
	Series I		Series II	
	d_1: FD (fPw)	d_2: WD (wPf)	d_1: FD (fPw)	d_2: WD (wPf)
a_1: entering goalbox (g)	− o_1: food, shock	+ o_2: water	+ o_2: food	− o_1: water, shock
a_2: abstaining from entering goalbox (α_g)	+ o_2: ω	− o_1: ω	− o_1: ω	+ o_2: ω

Note: different animals were run in Series I and Series II.

Here, FD and WD function to arouse *fPw* and *wPf*, respectively, but the act-outcome expectancies are the *same* under the two conditions. Putting it into common language, the animals did not need to discriminate one preference from the other in order to tell how to get food or how to get water; the outcomes were not differentially contingent upon the preferences. This difference between the experiments of Hull and Leeper becomes visible in the mechanics of the procedures when one notes that Hull had to change between food and water in the goalbox and also had to move the barrier from one side to the other on different trials, depending upon the subject's deprivation states, whereas Leeper's conditions were constant for a given subject in a given Series. The former is characteristic of discrimination experiments and the latter of expectancy experiments.

Cheng's Experiment

Cheng (1960) employed several procedures, of which we shall describe one that is of interest here because it contrasts in a number of features with the foregoing illustrations. In this procedure his rats were trained to run down a straight alley, jump a hurdle, and enter a goalbox in which they obtained either a pellet of food, if they were under FD, or access to a water bottle, if they were under WD. They were then given 100 trials during which the same conditions held, with the addition that half of the rats (those of Series I) were shocked in the goalbox when they were under FD and made contact with the food and half (those of Series II) were shocked in the goalbox when they were under WD and made contact with the water. The conditions of these 100 trials are represented in Table 9.5. As the table indicates, the rats of Series I learned to enter the goalbox when they were under WD but not to do so when they were under FD, and those of Series II learned to enter the goalbox when under FD but not to do so when under WD.

If we construe the experimental situation as involving the alternative acts of entering the goalbox (g) and abstaining from entering this box (α_g), the situation may be interpreted as follows. FD and WD arouse the preference states fPw and wPf, respectively, which function as discriminanda. Under FD, the subjects desire food (*i.e.*, $fP\omega$) and under WD they desire water (*i.e.*, $wP\omega$). However, regardless of their states of deprivation, they are averse to the combination of food and shock, *i.e.*, $wP(f,sh)$ and to the combination of water and shock, *i.e.*, $\omega P(w,sh)$. The formulas for the choices in Series I at the end of training are then:

$$\text{under } d_1 \text{ [FD } (fPw)]:\ \alpha_g * [\omega P(f,sh) \wedge \alpha_g gE\omega \wedge g\alpha_g E(f,sh)];$$

$$\text{under } d_2 \text{ [WD } (wPf)]:\ g * (wP\omega \wedge g\alpha_g Ew \wedge \alpha_g gE\omega).$$

The corresponding formulas for Series II are:

$$\text{under } d_1 \text{ [FD } (fPw)]:\ g * (fP\omega \wedge g\alpha_g Ef \wedge \alpha_g gE\omega);$$

$$\text{under } d_2 \text{ [WD } (wPf)]:\ \alpha_g * [(\omega P(w,sh)) \wedge \alpha_g gE\omega \wedge g\alpha_g E(w,sh)].$$

Note that in each group of subjects, at least one of the motivating preferences for the choices, namely, $\omega P(f,sh)$ in Series I and $\omega P(w,sh)$ in

Series II, is distinct from the preferences that function as discriminanda, whether these are taken to be fPw and wPf, as in the table, or (as is quite defensible) $fP\omega$ and $wP\omega$.

Bolles and Petrinovich's Experiment

Although the subjects of Leeper's experiment learned more rapidly than those of Hull's experiment, Bolles and Petrinovich (1954) believed that they could arrange conditions for even more efficient learning. They used a maze in which the rat's living cage was the starting box, with a door on each side leading to an alley and goalbox. For any particular rat, food was always on one side and water on the other, and the rats were given experience, including correction trials, that provided an opportunity for them to develop appropriate act-outcome expectancies, say, $rlEf$ and $lrEw$. It was found that they quickly learned to go to the food side when under FD and to the water side when under WD. From the present point of view, this, like Leeper's experiment, is in the form of a standard act-outcome experiment, not a discrimination experiment; the differential outcomes were not contingent upon the animals' states of preference. The results show that the appropriate act-outcome expectancies were acquired and exhibited, but do not tell us anything about discrimination between the states induced by FD and WD.[1]

Comments by S–R Theorists

The inconclusiveness of the design used by Leeper and by Bolles and Petrinovich for the problem of "drive discrimination" has not gone unnoticed by S–R psychologists, who have pointed out that the results might be predicted by a Tolmanian or "expectancy" theory. They themselves tend to introduce the S–R analog to expectancy, the "fractional anticipatory response," into their accounts of such results. This can be seen, for example, in Kendler's (1946) discussion of his own experiment and in Webb's (1955) review of work on "drive stimuli as cues." Osgood (1953, p. 418ff.) offers a particularly clear treatment of the problem, presenting both a Tolmanian view involving expectancies and an S–R hypothesis that relies upon mediation by anticipatory responses.

The difficulties encountered by such S–R hypotheses have been described by the authors just cited, as well as by others (*e.g.*, Deutsch,

1956). Inasmuch as the intention here is to present a relatively formalized cognitive view rather than to criticize S–R theory, we shall not comment on these difficulties, but restrict ourselves to brief consideration of two objections offered by S–R theorists against a Tolmanian position.

a. Webb (1955, p. 291) correctly says of applications of cognitive theory to these problems, "The opponents of this theory are likely to state that this hypothesis is merely a restatement of what the animal did and has little functional value as an hypothesis." Such an objection is indeed common, and is no doubt cogent against mere *ad hoc* cognitive accounts of particular sets of results. It is hoped that one virtue of the present formalization is its showing how to assess each of the explanatory processes independently and without circular reference to the behavior that is to be explained.

b. After reviewing experimental work on latent learning, "drive discrimination," and learning under "irrelevant" motivation and reward, Osgood (1953, p. 422) comments, "The really puzzling thing in both Hull and Tolman theories is the failure of effective representing processes to appear in some of these experiments." We do not take issue with this statement itself; such puzzling cases do exist. The puzzle arises from the fact that learning fails to appear under circumstances that seemed to the theorist to be favorable for it. This may, of course, mean that the theory is wrong, but it may also mean only that the conditions of learning are not sufficiently understood or are not in fact realized in the experiment, contrary to appearances. Osgood himself makes this clear. Only an ideally complete theory could specify both the necessary and *sufficient* conditions for learning or any other process. The SAO view is that expectancies as defined in its scheme are observed facts, and no more hypothetical than any other facts. The question then is not whether they exist, but whether they are useful for a science of psychology.

Were States Discriminated?

Granting that the experiments of Besch *et al.*, Jenkins and Hanratty, Hull, and Cheng conformed to the standard discrimination experiment and produced positive results, there remains the question, what were the effective discriminanda? In particular, can it be maintained that they were differential preference states?

If preference states are behavioral dispositions for which the fundamental evidence is that provided by standard preference experiments, it follows that an *experimenter* can discriminate between such states in an organism by means of the results of appropriate diagnostic experiments (*cf.* Note 2), but (unless he has such data available and can understand them) a *subject* can at best discriminate between secondary criteria of the states, that is, variables that are not the states themselves but are valid indicators of them.

Conditions of FD and WD and of satiation for food or water are commonly used with confidence that they will induce typically different preference states, such as are implied by the words "hunger" and "thirst." Such confidence rests upon a large body of experience and experiment, which could be embodied in a low-order empirical law to the effect that, in the case of rats, desires to eat and drink increase in strength with deprivation of food or water up to at least some such period as 24 to 48 hours, and that these states can be reduced or abolished by appropriate feeding and drinking. This loose generalization is not questioned here; it is supposed that the rats of the experiments cited in this chapter were indeed in the states of fPw, wPf, or, in Jenkins and Hanratty's experiments, two different strengths of $fP\omega$.

Unhappily, as the smallest acquaintance with the contemporary literature on hunger and thirst makes evident, the effects of FD and WD are extremely numerous and complex, both psychologically and physiologically. New facts about peripheral and central mechanisms related to these states are constantly being reported. Although changes in preference states are among the most marked and regular of the psychological phenomena that vary with deprivation, the task of discovering what differential cues are closely related to these preferences, what ones are not, and which out of all the existing possibilities an animal uses in such experiments as we have been discussing has scarcely begun. In some experiments it is possible that the deprivation and satiation operations might themselves provide differential cues: for example, a rat might have particles of food in its mouth in a trial under food-satiation but not under water-satiation; a water bottle might be present in the home cage just before a trial under water-satiation but not under food-satiation. In addition, some experimenters have strictly alternated FD and WD from day to day, thus jeopardizing independence of trials. Such difficulties have received less attention in the research and reviews than might be expected, although, as matters of experimental control, they are significant regardless of one's theoretical orientation.

Perhaps the strongest assertion about rats' ability to discriminate among their own states that can reasonably be made at the present time is that they can discriminate between variables associated with FD and

WD, but that little or nothing is known as to what the effective discriminanda are. As will be shown in Chapter 10, it is now possible to induce hunger and thirst, or preference states concerned with eating and drinking, by electrical and chemical stimulation of the brain, thus eliminating some of the confounding factors associated with deprivation and satiation (though no doubt at the cost of introducing new complexities). Stutz, Butcher, and Rossi (1969) have made a beginning in the study of rats' discriminations of such stimulation at loci that differ in their rewarding properties. It is apparent, however, that statements in this chapter concerning the functions of preference states as discriminanda are tentative, at best.

Work on the capacity of *human beings* to discriminate among their own psychological states has scarcely begun. Schachter and Singer (1962, p. 395) offer experimental evidence that:

> . . . given a state of physiological arousal for which an individual has no explanation, he will label this state in terms of the cognitions available to him. This implies, of course, that by manipulating the cognitions of an individual in such a state we can manipulate his feelings in diverse directions.

Although we fail to see why the first statement is said to imply the second, there is no doubt that Schachter and Singer's subjects gave differential reports of their emotional states of "euphoria" and "anger," and exhibited differential "emotional expression" in their behavior when they were given different information to account for the physiological arousal produced by injections of epinephrin. Similarly, Schachter has reviewed a variety of evidence to support the view that obese persons do not discriminate between hunger and such other states as anger and anxiety and therefore ". . . may not know when they are physiologically hungry" (Schachter, 1968, p. 751). This is consonant with earlier findings of Stunkard and Koch (1964) and Griggs and Stunkard (1964) that obese persons showed stronger "biases" than nonobese persons in the relation between their reported hunger and their recorded gastric motility.

SUMMARY

An organism's own psychological states constitute possible discriminanda for its behavior. A considerable body of experimental literature has studied the question whether such an animal as the rat can discriminate between its own states of hunger and thirst, or, in SAO language, between the states fPw and wPf. These states have usually been induced in such experiments by procedures of FD, WD, and satiation for food and water. Positive results have been obtained from standard discrimination experiments in which the subjects' obtaining of a preferred differential outcome was contingent upon their use of some variable or variables differentially associated with FD and WD, or with two different periods of FD. At the present time, however, it is by no means clear what these effective variables are, and it is risky to assume that they are necessarily valid indicators of the preference states. Hence, the question whether the rat can discriminate between such states is still open. Little work on this problem has yet been done with human subjects.

It was pointed out that some experiments that are often cited as "drive discrimination" experiments are not discrimination experiments at all, but have the form of standard act-outcome expectancy experiments.

NOTES AND COMMENTS

1. The discussion of the contrast between Hull's experiment and those of Leeper and of Bolles and Petrinovich should make it plain that it is not the use of a correction method as such that turns an intended discrimination experiment into an expectancy experiment. There are two types of correction procedures, in one of which (like Hull's), an incorrect choice does not provide the subject with information concerning the whereabouts of the dispreferred outcome on that trial, whereas in the other (like those of Leeper and of Bolles and Petrinovich), an incorrect choice does provide such information (given, of course, that the rat runs all the way to the goalbox). One might ask, why not use a correction procedure like Leeper's, but shift the food and water from one side to the other in accordance with the deprivation state, so as to force the rat to use the resulting preference states as discriminanda, thus turning the experiment into a proper discrimination experiment? It is amusing to notice that this would work out in such a way that the preferred outcome, whether food or water, would now always be on the same side, and the dispreferred outcome on the other side. For example, in Series I of Leeper's experiment (Table 9.4), food would be on the right when the animal was hungry and water would be on the right when the animal was thirsty; hence the rat should turn right regardless of the deprivation conditions, and the

experiment would be a special type of "generalized expectancy" experiment. This peculiar difficulty comes from trying to employ the same preference states both as discriminanda and as the motivating states for the choices. It would not arise in the procedure of Besch *et al.*, if this were modified to permit the animal to find the dispreferred outcome (ω) on an incorrect choice and then to retrace to the correct side to find the social rat. The procedure would still be a discrimination experiment, because the rat could make consistently correct choices only by using the states resulting from FD and WD as discriminanda. Oddly enough, as exemplified by an experiment by Bolles (1962), if the animal is required to use two different intensities of the same state (in this case, hunger) as discriminanda, these states can be used also as the motivating states and a full correction procedure can be employed, and yet the experiment is a proper discrimination experiment. Here, the placement of food in one box or the other varies with the intensities of hunger, so that the latter constitute genuine discriminanda for the choices.

2. In the text statement about the experimenter's ability to discriminate between two different states of an organism by means of standard diagnostic experiments, the term "discriminate" is intended in its strict sense. For example, a graduate student of psychology might be examined for his ability to discriminate between two states of a rat, say, *fPw* and *wPf*. He is given the same rat on each of a sufficiently large number of occasions, the animal being in the states *fPw* and *wPf* equally often in random order over the occasions. (It is the examiner's responsibility to see to it that the animal is in these states.) The student is required to invent and perform the appropriate standard preference experiments and to judge after getting the data on each occasion which of the two states is present. The examiner would tell the student on each occasion whether his judgment was correct or incorrect. These judgments would be in binary form and would constitute the data from which the examiner would determine whether the student had succeeded in discriminating between the two states.

The examination is in the form of a standard discrimination experiment. The discriminanda are the two states of the rat; the alternative acts are the student's judgments *"fPw"* and *"wPf"*; the differential outcomes are the examiner's saying "correct" and "incorrect." (The fact that the student must engage in much activity between each presentation of a discriminandum—the rat in one or the other of the two states—and his choice between the alternative acts merely means that this process of discrimination is different and much more

complex than an ordinary "sensory" discrimination.) A reversal procedure is available, but awkward and presumably unnecessary—it would
require the student to report *"fPw"* when the rat was in *wPf* and *"wPf"*
when it was in *fPw*. (This foolish procedure could be avoided by the
student's use of some pair of arbitrary acts, such as pressing one of two
keys for *fPw* and the other for *wPf;* the significance of the keys could
be reversed without generating a conflict with normal use of language.)

Note that the student would exhibit discrimination between the
two states of the rat even if he were rebellious and preferred being told
he was incorrect to being told he was correct. The results would be the
reverse of what the examiner had expected but they would still answer
the original question. The examiner under these conditions would have
the right to fail the student only if he had asked for identification of
the states, which requires discrimination but goes beyond it. (If the
student was sophisticated and wished to spoil the experiment, he would
act at random by means of a chance device.)

3. The present chapter by no means constitutes a review of the
literature on "drive discrimination." Numerous additional references can
be found in the reviews by Webb (1955), Cofer and Appley (1964), and
Bolles (1967).

10

Preferences among States

Just as we may ask whether an organism can discriminate among its own states (Chapter 9), so we may ask whether it has preferences among these states. It is generally supposed that some states are desired, some are neutral, and some are aversive. Motivational and emotional states, especially, such as hunger, thirst, sexual arousal, fear, and frustration, are believed to be marked by preference value, sometimes of the most intense sort. A straightforward test of such beliefs is to use these states, together with ω, as differential outcomes in standard preference experiments.

As in the parallel case of discrimination, a small and rather specialized literature has developed around this problem. The meagerness of the work testifies in part to the practical difficulties of manipulating states as differential outcomes, but recently discovered techniques of inducing "hunger" and other states by electrical stimulation (ES) of hypothalamic regions of the brain have enabled some progress to be made.

PREFERENCE VALUE OF THE DESIRE FOR FOOD

If it is possible to induce a state of desire for food $(fP\omega)$[1] by ES of the lateral hypothalamus, a standard preference experiment can test whether the organism desires $fP\omega$, is neutral toward it, or is aversive to it, by making $fP\omega$ and ω the differential outcomes of alternative acts in the presence of appropriately selected discriminanda. Such an experiment was performed for illustrative purposes by Rose (1968) and is represented in Table 10.1.[2] An albino rat was prepared with an electrode aimed at the lateral hypothalamus. The animal was maintained with *ad lib.* access to food and water. In pre- and post-tests, ES induced feeding within an average of 4 sec. The animal was run in a T-maze with a lamp above the choice-point; the light was on (d_1) and off (d_2) in a random order over

Table 10.1
Preference value of desire for food ($fP\omega$) in an
albino rat (Rose, 1968)

	Situations			
	Series I		Series II	
	d_1: light off	d_2: light on	d_1: light off	d_2: light on
a_1: turns right	+ o_1: ES ($fP\omega$)	− o_2: ω	− o_2: ω	+ o_1: ES ($fP\omega$)
a_2: turns left	− o_2: ω	+ o_1: ES ($fP\omega$)	+ o_1: ES ($fP\omega$)	− o_2: ω

trials. In Series I, turning right in the presence of d_1 and left in the presence of d_2 led to 20 sec. of ES in the goalbox, whereas turning left in the presence of d_1 and right in the presence of d_2 led to 20 sec. of confinement in the box without ES or other explicit differential outcomes. In Series II, which was run after the completion of Series I, reversal conditions held as indicated in the table. Trials were massed, the intertrial interval being approximately 5 sec. The table indicates the results of the last 50 of 100 trials in Series I and the last 50 of 75 trials in Series II; choices of the act leading to ES were made in 63 to 81 percent of these trials under the four conditions, the overall percentage being 75. The results for each of the two series were reliable at beyond the .01 level by chi-square tests. It is concluded that the animal desired ES or something associated with ES; whether it desired $fP\omega$, i.e., whether ($fP\omega$)$P\omega$, requires further consideration.

PROBLEMS OF RESEARCH ON PREFERENCES AMONG STATES

The principal difficulty of interpreting experiments on preferences among states is that of diagnosing precisely the objects of preference. This problem arises for two reasons: first, because in practice it is more difficult to identify psychological states of the organism than it is to identify most of the external objects and events that are employed as objects of preference; and, second, because the experimental manipulations that are designed to alter the states are likely, even when successful, to produce confounding effects in addition to those intended. Both difficulties will be recognized as having arisen in connection with the problem of *discriminating* among states.

Consider Rose's illustrative experiment. If we knew that ES of the hypothalamus had the effect of inducing a desire for food, and if we also knew that the presence and absence of this desire were the only differential outcomes of the rat's choices in the discrimination box, then the conclusion that the desire for food was itself desirable, *i.e.*, that $(fP\omega)P\omega$, would be firm. Let us consider the evidence on both points.

First, what can be said about the question whether such ES produces a desire for food? There is substantial support for the claim that this desire is indeed induced by such stimulation of certain regions of the lateral hypothalamus. Margules and Olds (1962) found that food-satiated rats, with some electrode placements, started to eat within two seconds of the onset of stimulation and stopped eating as soon as the shock was terminated. Hoebel and Teitelbaum (1962) reported similar results from electrical and chemical stimulation in the same region in rats. Mendelson and Chorover (1965) and Coons, Levak, and Miller (1965) showed that satiated rats learned a discrimination and a discrimination reversal under continuous ES with differential outcomes of food and ω; these experiments fitted the standard form of Chapter 3 for establishing the existence of a desire for food. The latter authors were able to go so far as to show transfer of such learning from the condition of continuous electrical stimulation to a condition of food deprivation. ES and food deprivation were shown by Tenen and Miller (1964) to have similar effects on thresholds of acceptability to rats of milk adulterated with quinine. The animals tolerated more quinine the greater the FD and the stronger the current, and the threshold values were in the same range; and the thresholds were higher when shock was given in addition to FD than for the FD or shock alone—a "summation" effect. That these effects were not a matter of general activation was indicated by their absence when WD and water adulterated with quinine were substituted for FD and quinine in milk. Thus, there is little doubt that a desire for food can be induced by hypothalamic stimulation.

Secondly, granted that ES has this effect, is this its *only* effect? It would be surprising if this were the case, considering the nonbiological nature of such stimulation and its gross character, even with the best experimental control, as contrasted with what one supposes must be the elaborate and delicate arrangements of normal brain functioning. Coons, Levak, and Miller (1965), in the paper cited above, observed that the transfer of discrimination learning from conditions of ES to those of FD was not perfect, and their cautionary statement is significant:

> ... there may be a great stimulus-generalization decrement from the effects of ESLH [electrical stimulation of the lateral hypothalamus] to normal hunger, since the ESLH state to which learning was presumably conditioned probably involves many cues other than those of hunger, such as cues associated with sexual drive, sleep, thirst, temperature, and other functions that the lateral hypothalamus may also subserve. (p. 1321)

Although the theoretical language differs from that used here, the point is valid; and it might be strengthened by imagining various effects of "normal" FD that may not be produced by ES. It is remarkable that the effects of hypothalamic stimulation run as nearly parallel to those of FD as they have been shown to do.

As a parallel to arousal of a desire for food by ES, it may be noted that Roberts and Carey (1965) were able to demonstrate that what they called a "readiness to gnaw" was induced by ES in the mediolateral hypothalamus of rats. Positive results were obtained in several test situations, including learning and reversal of a black-white discrimination in a Y-maze, the differential outcomes of the choices being the opportunity to gnaw a wood or cardboard object *vs.* ω. Controls indicated that the state induced was not a desire for food, a desire for exploration, or a state of general activation. The gnawing did not occur as a "vacuum act" in the absence of appropriate objects.

Returning to the interpretation of Rose's experiment, it seems likely that his rat's choices of ES did in fact have the outcome of arousing in it the state $fP\omega$. The electrode was implanted in or near the lateral hypothalamic regions in which ES has been shown to have this effect. In tests both before and after the choice experiment, the rat showed the "stimulus-bound" feeding to ES that has generally been taken to be evidence of hunger, and therefore of $fP\omega$, although during the whole experiment it was maintained on *ad lib.* food and water.

Nevertheless, it would be risky to conclude from Table 10.1 that Rose's subject was displaying a desire for the state $fP\omega$. As is often the case with such electrode placements, under noncontingent ES the animal showed not only stimulus-bound feeding in the presence of food, but also tendencies, less well-marked, to drink in the presence of water and to gnaw in the presence of gnawable materials, although each of these tendencies was overriden by the feeding tendency when food was available. It is therefore possible that the choice of ES as a differential outcome indicated a desire for the states of a desire for water or a desire to gnaw, rather than for a desire for food; or, since these states are not incompatible with each other, the intended objects of the choices could have been any combination of them. That the animal desired some consequence of ES is clear, but the identification of the object of desire remains in doubt. It seems likely that such identification will come about only gradually through the convergence of various lines of evidence as research proceeds.

Even a conclusion as weak as this, however, is disturbing to proponents of a "drive" conception of motivation, especially when this is linked with a drive-reduction theory of "reinforcement." According to such a position, organisms will tend to learn to reduce and escape from drive states, since whatever they do that has these effects will tend to become habitual in the circumstances under which it happens. Nothing in such a theory prepares one for the phenomenon of an organism that actually desires to be hungry or thirsty or sexually aroused or frightened; on the contrary, drive states as envisaged by such theorists, of whom Hull (1943) has been, of course, the most influential, must clearly be classified as aversive. The problem is put succinctly by Mendelson and Chorover (1965, p. 560):

> Thus, the main finding of our experiment is that lateral hypothalamic stimulation which induces eating in satiated rats can also serve as a motivational condition for the learning of a new response to obtain food in a T-maze. In this respect, lateral hypothalamic stimulation has the same motivational effects as normal hunger induced by food deprivation. However, the effects of stimulation differ from those of food deprivation in that the minimum current intensity required to induce eating is also positively reinforcing.

But perhaps the minimal FD required for eating *is* "reinforcing" (in our terms, desired); the writer knows of no contrary evidence. It appears that Mendelson and Chorover, like many other psychologists, are so well convinced of the validity of a drive-reduction hypothesis of learning that they infer the aversiveness of normal hunger from the fact that animals do eat when hungry, that eating does reduce hunger, and that learning to get food does take place. But if this theory of learning is given up, one may look at the facts without partiality, and ask whether "normal hunger" is aversive or neutral or desired. Facts leading toward the last of these alternatives would then not be embarrassing.

Against the conception that a desire to eat may be desired might be urged the argument that, at the human level, a person may want to be hungry enough to enjoy eating and for this reason will take measures to improve his appetite if it fails. In this case, the desire to eat might be neutral or even to some degree aversive, as long as the aversiveness was counterbalanced sufficiently by the "pleasures of eating."[3] Such an argument distinguishes between the desiredness of the state of desiring to eat and the desire that eating shall be desirable; in other words, the state of desiring to eat is thought of as "intrinsically" neutral or aversive, but as having also a secondary or derived desirability as a means to a desired end, that of eating. This distinction is in no way repugnant to the present position, but it is clear that the decisive experiments will not be easy to develop. Rose's rat showed a desire for electrical stimulation of the hypothalamus that was not in fact followed by the outcome of eating; but, on the one hand, the rat was experienced in the relation between hunger and eating and, on the other, it is possible that extensive experimenting might show an eventual loss of desirability of such stimulation if it were never followed by eating. It would be interesting to know whether electrical stimulation of the hypothalamus would be desired by animals that had been prevented from gaining experience of the relation of hunger to eating, as, perhaps, by intragastric feeding from infancy.

The aversiveness of intense hunger can hardly be doubted, even by those of us who have never been subjected to it. Although endemic partial starvation is said to be more likely to result in apathy than in riot and revolution, resort to criminality for the purpose of obtaining food is far from rare and may extend to cannibalism under some circumstances, as described by Keys *et al.* (1950). The report by the same authors on the behavior of their volunteer subjects under months of semistarvation is persuasive evidence for the aversiveness of this state, if such evidence is needed. It is quite possible, or even probable, that the affective value of the desire, like that of other conditions, is a function of its intensity, and that it is desired at low intensities and aversive at high intensities. It is well known that hypothalamic stimulation that is desired at low current values may become aversive if the current is intensified, although this fact is not decisive for the point.

Finally, the distinction between *hunger* and *appetite* as drawn, for example, by Cannon (1934), has too often been lost sight of in spite of the efforts of hedonic theorists like Young (1936, 1941, 1959, 1961, etc.). In the present context it may be worth while to take the risk of suggesting that normal food deprivation has at least dual effects, that of arousing a desire to eat (appetite) and that of inducing an aversive complex state of hunger. It is then conceivable that hypothalamic stimulation induces appetite but not hunger.[4]

DRIVE

The concept of drive and the drive-reduction hypothesis of reinforcement are so deeply engraved in the thought of many psychologists that they are often taken for granted uncritically in spite of the erosion that the notion of drive has suffered in recent years [see, *e.g.*, Bolles (1958) and Campbell and Misanin (1969)] and the doubts about the drive-reduction hypothesis expressed even by one of its most tenacious adherents (Miller, 1963). Considering possible biological functions of behavior, it was not implausible for Hull (1943) to imagine that deprivation of food gives rise to an energizing state of drive, that the energized organism, if lucky, finds food, that eating the food reduces the drive, and that this drive reduction increases the likelihood that the organism will tend to repeat its successful behavior when similar circumstances next arise. Unhappily, this model, based largely upon experimental work with hungry rats, was extended over a large part of the animal kingdom, over the greater part of the psychology of motivation, and over all of the psychology of learning except (for some theorists) Pavlovian conditioning. It happens that rats are convenient subjects, and nothing is easier than to deprive them of food. The writer ventures to say that contemporary psychology would look very different if hunger did not exist and if, say, a rat's desire to play were as easy to arouse and to abolish as hunger is.

From an SAO point of view, the word "drive," if retained at all, should be understood to mean "any aversive emotional state." The present chapter has set forth the criteria of aversiveness of psychological states; the criteria of "emotionality" will be discussed in Chapter 12. The "energizing," but also the "depressing," characteristics of drive are its emotional properties, while the organism's tendency to avoid situations that arouse drive and to seek situations that reduce or eliminate it would reflect its aversiveness. The one-sidedness of this view would be compensated for by the conception of *desired* states, which may also be emotional and thus energizing or depressing, but whose arousal the organism will seek and whose reduction or elimination the organism will resist. Where intentional behavior is concerned, the learning that is required for seeking and avoidance is here presumed to be the acquisition and modification of act-outcome expectancies.

SUMMARY

States of the organism may be treated as objects of preference; their desiredness, neutrality, or aversiveness, like that of other objects, can be studied experimentally. Electrical stimulation of the lateral hypothalamus in the rat has been found to arouse a desire for food, and there is evidence that rats desire such stimulation. Precise identification of the object of preference in such cases has not, however, been achieved, since ES has other consequences besides the desire to eat, including, for example, a desire to drink and a desire to gnaw. Since the aversiveness of intense hunger resulting from prolonged semistarvation appears to be well established, it is possible, or even probable, that the desire for food is desired at low intensities and aversive at high intensities. It is also possible that the state produced by lateral hypothalamic ES is intrinsically neutral or aversive but acquires secondary desirability through its function of making the eating of food desirable. In any case, it is advantageous to deal with the affective value of motivational states as a matter open to experimental test, rather than to adopt a theoretical position like that of "drive theory," which requires such states to be aversive.

NOTES AND COMMENTS

1. Here, and occasionally elsewhere, a symbol of the form "oPo'" is to be read as a substantive, "the state of preferring o to o'," instead of as a sentence, "o is preferred to o'." Rather than introducing a new symbol for these instances, we rely upon the context to keep the distinction clear.

2. The writer is grateful to Mr. Mitchel Rose for obtaining these data for the purposes of the present chapter. He is not responsible, however, for the interpretation given them here.

3. In a study of the induction of *thirst* by hypothalamic electrical stimulation, Mendelson (1967) found that two of his three rats failed to press a lever that gave them this ES unless water was available to them for

drinking. Taken together with the fact that thirsty rats will press a lever for water, this led him to say (p. 1079), "Thus if the rat is given the thirst it will press for the water; if given the water it will press for the thirst."

4. Research on functions of the hypothalamus and related brain structures is proceeding so vigorously that our suppositions about these functions must be regarded as tentative. Furthermore, we have not even mentioned in the text the experimentally-supported view that hypothalamic ES has two separable consequences, a "drive" effect and a "reinforcement" effect, presumably due to stimulation of two different sets of neural structures. In SAO language, this amounts to saying that stimulation of one of these sets of structures is aversive or arouses an aversive state and that stimulation of the other set is desired. See, *e.g.*, Deutsch (1960), Gallistel (1964, 1967), Ball (1969), and, for a dissenting opinion, Trowill, Panksepp, and Gandelman (1969).

Since this chapter was written, Valenstein, Cox, and Kakolewski (1970) have argued that hypothalamic ES excites neural centers underlying, not drive states, but "well-established response patterns." If, for example, eating, gnawing, and carrying happen to be acts in such a pattern, then Valenstein *et al.* suggest that performing any one of these acts would discharge the underlying neural center and would thereby be "reinforcing" (*i.e.*, in SAO language, desired). The assumption that performance of an act may have preference value is alluded to elsewhere in this book (pp. 55, 81-82, and 168-169).

11

Some Problems of Intentional Behavior

This chapter is devoted to remarks and speculations on a number of problems of intentional behavior as seen from the point of view of an SAO system.

MOTIVATION AND COGNITION

The words "motive" and "motivation" are not technical terms in the system and therefore will not be defined. They may be used to refer loosely to matters concerned with preferences, just as "cognition" may be used to refer loosely to matters concerned with discrimination, expectancy, and other aspects of the acquisition and use of knowledge, when precision is either not possible or not aspired to. Thus, the preference in an interlocked triad may be thought of as the motivational element, and the complementary act-outcome expectancies as the cognitive elements, in the definition of an intentional act.

MOTIVES, GENERAL AND SPECIFIC

If a person is said to desire food, to desire achievement, or to be averse to chamber music, "food," "achievement," and "chamber music" are names of classes of differential outcomes, each class containing members as diverse from each other as soup from steak, as making a million dollars from winning a game of chess against a renowned player, or as a Haydn quartet from one by Schoenberg. Such general motives may be contrasted with highly specific ones that refer to classes that contain but a single member, such as a woman's desire to find her lost wedding ring or Person A's hatred of Person B. Here the object of desire or aversion is individualized; no other ring can become the lost wedding ring and no other person is substitutable as an object of the hatred borne to Person B. (*Cf.* Singer, 1923, on love as a sentiment that individuates.) The nature of the first sort of motives, *i.e.*, those concerned with classes having more than one member, is worth some analysis.

Desires for Foods

Consider a human being in a restaurant or a rat in a T-maze under conditions in which each of them may be said to "desire food." The human being believes that he can obtain food by ordering it, and the rat believes that it can obtain food by turning to the right and getting into the goalbox. If the human being orders filet mignon and is told that it is not available, he may indignantly march out to another restaurant, but it is more likely that he will order another item from the menu. If the rat finds wet mash in the goalbox instead of the customary dry pellet, it may show signs of surprise, but it will probably eat the mash and go to the same box on the next trial. In general, if an organism desires food, this means that the members of a large class of differential outcomes will be relatively high in its overall preference order at that moment; when the desire is reduced or eliminated, these objects will simultaneously fall to lower ranks, and under thorough satiation some of them may become aversive. Thus, the objects of a desire for food constitute a class of differential outcomes whose preference values are intercorrelated and which, so far as preference is concerned, are to some degree mutually substitutable.

At least from the time of Cannon (*e.g.*, 1934), the distinction between "hunger" and "appetite" has warned us not to suppose that foods constitute a single homogeneous class. This is obvious enough at the dinner table, where members of a subclass called "desserts" are differentially desirable according to whether or not a "main course" has already been eaten. In experimental work, the at least partially independent rewarding effects of oral and gastric stimulation—food in the mouth *vs.* food in the stomach—have been studied (*e.g.*, Miller and Kessen, 1952); some foods have mainly the one effect, some the other, and some both. The reader may consider for himself how far, and for what purposes, it is useful to pursue research into the structure of preferences among foods and the biological, individual, and social variables that affect this structure. It can be seen immediately, however, that organisms do not have to be as different as carnivores from herbivores, or as Eskimos from Hottentots, to have markedly different "desires for food" when such desires are defined, as here, by the individual organism's choices and not by such nonbehavioral criteria as physical and chemical constitution, nutritive value, and the like. Among human beings, at any rate, adult individuals' personal histories and social environments can be counted upon to specialize each person's food-preference structure.

If a pebble looks like a pellet to a rat and the animal desires it as if it were a pellet, the pebble has to count at that moment as a member of the class of intercorrelated differential outcomes, most of which, no doubt, would be edible. The fact that the pebble will probably drop out of the class as soon as the rat discovers its qualities does not mean that it was not formerly a member of the class. To say that the rat does not really desire the pebble, or to judge that some man does not really desire some woman, or to tell a child that he is not really afraid of the little dog, usually means, not that the desire or aversion does not exist, but rather that the object will fall out of the intercorrelated class if and when the subject has sufficient experience with it; such misbegotten desires and aversions are frequently only too real.

Specific Appetites

For some years, psychologists and biologists have been interested in the fact that organisms, including rats and human beings, appear to develop relatively specific desires for certain food elements (*e.g.*, salt, phosphorus, thiamine, etc.) if their diets have been deficient in these elements. The study of this phenomenon provides a minor object-lesson in the diagnosis of motivation. If a rat is fed a diet that lacks thiamine and thereupon prefers a new diet containing thiamine to the old diet, the animal has commonly been regarded as exhibiting a craving for thiamine. In the present context, it is notable that this natural-seeming hypothesis concerning the animal's motivation has been shown to be erroneous in a number of instances. Rozin and his students (*e.g.*, Rozin, 1967; Rozin and Rodgers, 1967) have produced strong evidence that a rat deprived of thiamine does not in fact prefer food with this element over food without it, but rather is aversive to the deficient diet upon which it has sickened; thus, the rat will choose a novel food, with or without thiamine, over the deficient one and will eat little if any of the deficient diet under conditions in which it will clearly show a desire for food if a new diet is made available. That the deficient diet is aversive, rather than merely less desired than usual, is suggested by the rats' gingerly approach to it and their tendency to spill it; here one relies upon the experienced observer's opinion that such behavior is shown only toward aversive foods. If the deficient diet is eaten at all when it is aversive, the presumption is that this is the resultant of conflict between the aversion to the diet and the desire to eat. Thus, Rozin's new solution of an old problem replaces the specific appetite for thiamine by an aversion to a diet associated with illness due to thiamine deficiency. Theories that have attempted to account for a thiamine-specific appetite must give way to a theory of an acquired aversion to food associated with illness; this connects naturally with the phenomena of rats' ability to learn to avoid poisons and their apparent differential tendency to associate the discomfort of illness produced by X-rays or poison with taste rather than auditory and visual stimulation (*e.g.*, Garcia and Koelling, 1966).

Achievement Motivation

Studies of "achievement motivation" have relied heavily upon projective methods (*e.g.*, McClelland *et al.*, 1953; Atkinson, 1958), which must be regarded as secondary, rather than fundamental, if such a thing as motivation toward achievement is to be defined in an SAO system. The question is quite analogous to questions concerning the existence of "desire for food," however different the objects of preference and the means whereby they have acquired preference value may be. What needs to be found is a class of objects that may reasonably be called "achievements," the preference values of which are intercorrelated over time and changes of conditions for an individual person. It can be expected that, as with desires for food, only some degree of overlap among such classes will occur from one person to another. Furthermore, in a case so obviously conditioned by personal history and social surroundings, the preference-structure can hardly be simple; the distinction now common between "desire for success" and "fear of failure" suggests the existence of at least two partially independent subclasses of achievements, and this is probably only a beginning. (See, *e.g.*, Birney, Burdick, and Teevan, 1969.) Whatever the merits of projective devices, they tend to lead to highly indirect validation of the psychological analyses that prompt them and that are prompted by them. Fundamental nonprojective studies of choices among outcomes characterized as achievements by the theory of achievement motivation might help to clarify the concept.

MOTIVES AND CONCEPTS

By the definitions of Chapter 6, the intended outcome of an intentional act is both the preferred and the expected member of a pair of differential outcomes, and thus is represented psychologically in both a motivational state, the preference, and a cognitive state, the expectancy. If more or less general motives exist, such as a desire for food or a desire for achievement, the classes of intercorrelated outcomes that define such general motives constitute something like what is commonly called a "concept." The preference states $o_1 P o_2$ and $o_3 P o_2$ differ from each other with respect to the objects o_1 and o_3; the same is true of the expectancy states $a_1 a_2 E o_1$ and $a_1 a_2 E o_3$. It is not assumed here that there is some sort of pictorial likeness between the objects of these states and externally defined instances of the objects, nor even that the organism necessarily has representations of the objects of cognition (*e.g.*, "ideas," "images," or the like) independent of the states of preference or expectancy that refer to them. Nevertheless, the psychologist who can talk about the preference states $o_1 P o_2$ and $o_3 P o_2$ can also talk about o_1, o_2, and o_3 as objects of these states and can distinguish among them experimentally. The present point is that experiments may require him to describe an outcome as a relatively narrowly defined class (*e.g.*, Purina Chow pellets of a certain weight) or as a relatively general class (*e.g.*, a class containing pellets, mash, sucrose solutions, sunflower seeds, etc.). It is in this special sense that we would agree with a statement by Brown (1965, p. 194): "In order to set a positive value on achievement and a negative value on aggression, for instance, one must possess the two concepts: achievement and aggression."

It is not always easy to determine the extent to which such a concept is represented in the organism itself, rather than only in the observer. No doubt it is reasonable to ascribe a desire for food, or more narrowly, a desire to eat dinner, to a human being as he enters a restaurant, in the sense that his chosen act of entering the restaurant is motivated by a desire, not for any particular foods, but for any of a large number of possible "dinner" foods; and it would be possible to find out what kinds of dinner foods he expected this choice to make available. But if a desire for "food" is ascribed to a rat when it chooses to turn right rather than left in a maze, it is questionable whether the observer has not attributed more generality to the object both of the preference and of the act-outcome expectancies than truly enters into the animal's choice, especially if the rat has always found, say, a Purina Chow pellet of a particular size in the goalbox and no other differential outcome. The "psychologist's fallacy" (James, 1890)—*i.e.*, confusing the observer's interpretation with the psychological state that is being interpreted—is exceedingly difficult to avoid in talking about an organism's motivation.

Imagine a person who, having inserted the appropriate coins in a cigarette vending machine, pulls the lever marked for Brand A and finds that the machine is empty of this brand. If his choice was motivated by a desire for "a pack of cigarettes," he may be expected to pull one lever after another, perhaps in the order of decreasing preference value of the various brands, until a pack of cigarettes of some brand appears. If, on the other hand, his desire was for "a pack of Brand A cigarettes," and no more general than this, he would be expected to desist from pulling levers and to push the button to get his money back. Similarly, a man who, although rebuffed by one woman after another, is finally accepted by a woman and marries her will be said to have wanted desperately "to get married"; whereas a man who remains unmarried the rest of his life, after one rejection, may be thought to have wanted not merely to get married but to marry the particular woman who rejected him. The latter hypothesis would be strengthened if, late in his life, the woman relented and they were married, and all the more so if he had shunned numerous opportunities in the meanwhile. Even then (for the problem is not an easy one), the woman might be the only one the man had ever met who had blue eyes and black hair, which happened to be critical for his desire.

If the object of a general desire or aversion must be thought of as a form of concept, not merely for the observer, but for the organisms to which it is correctly ascribed, then it is clearly impossible for an organism to have a desire for something of which it cannot form such a concept. For example, in the discussion of the work of Myer and White (1965) on the desirability to a rat of an opportunity to kill a mouse (Ch. 6), it was commented that a rat could hardly be thought to desire the *death* of a mouse. The concept of death is hard enough for expert human beings themselves to define, as witness the questions arising in connection with transplantation of hearts, kidneys, and other organs of the body. Even if rats choose opportunities to kill mice and do in fact kill them (by the observer's definition of killing), the rats' preferred and expected outcomes cannot be coextensive as a class with what the observer himself would mean by killing (and equally, by the way, no animal but the human being can be supposed to have an aversion to death). The same can be said, for that matter, of the class referred to as "mice." A rat can speak about this for itself only by its choices; the observer has the advantage of language, but the conventional meaning of his words is seldom precisely applicable to the world of another organism, even that of another human being.

Every statement in this book about the objects of organisms' discriminations, preferences, and expectancies is subject to this imprecision. There is no way to eliminate such errors altogether, but their deleterious effects may be minimized if the student understands both that they exist and why they exist.

IMPOSSIBLE OUTCOMES

A puzzle arises from what seems to be the obvious fact that human beings can intend to achieve outcomes that are inachievable. According to Greenblatt (1965) a bill was laid before the Indiana State legislature in 1897 which, among other things, asserted that the area of a circle is equal to that of a square whose side is one-fourth of the circumference of the circle, which implies that π equals 4. The author of the bill claimed that he had "solutions of the trisection of the angle, duplication of the cube, and quadrature of the circle, which will be recognized as problems which have long since been given up by scientific bodies as unsolvable mysteries, and above man's ability to comprehend" (Greenblatt, 1965, p. 427A). The reader must be referred to the cited article for the history of this matter but will be relieved to learn that, after having been passed unanimously in the House, the bill was sent to the Committee on Temperance (*sic*) of the Senate and finally failed. Ludicrous as this example may be, it would be an odd conception of intention that denied that anyone can intend to solve a problem that has been shown by mathematicians to be incapable of solution, even though, in such a case, to assert a solution is to involve oneself in a self-contradiction. Other cases involve different kinds of impossibility, such as attempts to manufacture perpetual-motion machines, or attempts to accomplish something for which a necessary condition is absent, such as looking for gold in a mine in which in fact there is no gold, or attempts to do something patently beyond one's capacity, although not impossible in a more theoretical sense, such as running 100 yards in three seconds.

The question is not whether an organism can intend to perform an impossible task but, rather, how can we know that it has such an intention? The difficulty stems from the fact that an impossible outcome cannot be used as a differential outcome in a preference or expectancy experiment. To show that Moos preferred food tokens to worthless tokens (Chapter 3), Moos's choices were shown to depend upon his actually obtaining one or the other kind of token. But a desire to square the circle cannot be ascertained by an experiment in which the subject's acts sometimes have this outcome and sometimes do not.

The solution obviously has to proceed along the lines of the diagnostic rules of Chapter 7. If a rat goes to an empty box in which it has always previously found food, we do not take its failure to find food on this occasion as evidence against its desiring food. Rule I tells us that if the act was intentional and depended upon appropriate expectancies concerning this act and its alternative, then the act is evidence of a desire for food whether or not food was actually obtained. This kind of argument appears to be sufficient for such cases as searching for gold in a goldless mine or undertaking to run 100 yards in three seconds; one presumes that the behavior depends upon expectancies appropriate to the desire to find gold or to lower the world's record for the dash. It is necessary, however, to suppose that the expectancies, however they were acquired, have been generalized to the present situation, in which they happen to be unwarranted, and this takes us beyond any principles that have been asserted in the previous chapters. Furthermore, the expectancies must be assessed by the observer through indirect means, such as observing that the subject's choices of means support these hypotheses about his expected ends: the subject does whatever he has done in the past when he was known to be searching for gold.

In other cases, when previous successes in the same sort of undertaking are in principle unavailable, it is necessary to rely upon evidence still less direct. A principal form of such evidence is that of the wager. The hypothesis that a person intends to run 100 yards in three seconds would be supported by his betting a large sum of money upon this outcome at unfavorable odds. The same can be said about attempts to build perpetual-motion machines or to square the circle, if the unfortunate subject is seen to invest a material part of his time and energy in activities that would pay off only if the impossible were achieved. The fact that the outcomes are impossible puts the person in no different state than that of mathematicians and physicists who made similar attempts before the impossibilities were proved or recognized, except that he may be regarded as either ignorant or incompetent. If today someone is trying to produce a map that requires five colors, and tomorrow it is proved for the first time that four colors are enough for any map, the latter fact cannot be taken as evidence against the existence of the former. Similarly, before Arrow's (1951) monograph was published, someone may have instituted a group (committee, club, kibbutz) with rules such that, in his belief, the decisions of the group would reflect democratically the preferences of the members of the group. But there exists a particular small set of rules, each of which appears on the surface to be reasonable and desirable for the purpose; and if he happened to choose these rules, he unknowingly set up a group in which some decisions would be either "imposed or dictatorial" (Luce and Raiffa, 1957, p. 339). Should he be said not to have tried to be democratic?

RELATIONS BETWEEN SITUATIONS AND OUTCOMES

In Chapter 3, preference was treated as a relation between a pair of outcomes made up of differential outcomes in a c.o.f. It is now necessary to consider certain relations between these outcomes and the situation of the organism prior to its choice.

In some choices, the organism's situation after it has acted is largely the same as it was before the act except for the occurrence of a particular differential outcome. This might be true, for instance, of a person's decision to read one book rather than another, to invite one person rather than another to spend the evening with him, or to order one item rather than another from a menu in a restaurant. But other choices make for more general changes between the situations before and after the act, such as changing one's vocation rather than going on as usual, getting married rather than remaining single, and going away to college rather than being a commuter student. In the first kind of case, the c.p.f. and the c.o.f. may be similar or even identical to each other, whereas in the second kind, the c.p.f. and the c.o.f. may be quite different. At the level of our illustrative animal experiments, Moos could open either of the two panels without effecting any general change in his situation, but Lashley's rats, by jumping to either door, went from a small platform facing the two windows into one of two situations that differed both from the prior situation and from each other: either they landed on the other side of the window and received food or they bumped their noses on the locked window and fell into a net below.

The organism's motivation in the latter sort of case is likely to be more complex than might first appear. A student who is choosing among various colleges may be moved by a preference for the merits of the various colleges as he sees them; but if one of them is in his home town and the others are at a distance, the former will have special status according to his views of the advantages and disadvantages of his being near his home and the influences of his family and present friends. In the case of rats in a Lashley jumping apparatus, the animal may choose to abstain from jumping, rather than take the risks of the jump; for this reason, it has been a common procedure to have compressed air available to blow uncomfortably at the animal to motivate its jumping. In the special cases in which an experimenter wishes to make a subject choose between two aversive outcomes, it is necessary for him to make the prior situation aversive enough to guarantee that the choice will occur.

From this point of view, then, if a subject prefers his present situation to either of two outcomes that are presented for choice, the choice may not be made; rather, the subject is likely to choose to abstain from acting, thus exhibiting his preference for continued presence of the prior situation over a change to either of the two outcomes. If by some means the prior situation is rendered less preferable, then a two-stage decision-process may occur: first, a choice to leave the present field rather than remain in it and, second, a choice between the alternatives that are open if he leaves the present field. If both choices express themselves in the same act, as when a rat jumps both to get away from the discomfort of the compressed air and to get to the food rather than to bump his nose and fall, the motivation may not be clear to the observer and will require more subtle procedures of analysis. These difficulties arise, for example, when one attempts to assess Maier's (1949) claim that locking *both* windows of the jumping apparatus and forcing the rats to jump causes the animals to adopt stereotyped "fixated" acts that are unintentional or, in his language, "behavior without a goal."

COMPLEX INTENTIONAL ACTS AND INTENDED OUTCOMES

Complex Intentional Acts

An intended outcome can usually be achieved in more than one way, with various probabilities of success. To make a baby smile, smiling at him or wiggling fingers at him or emitting cooing sounds might be successful, even if the combination of all three acts made him cry. (Compare the discussion of Formula (5.3).)

Given that a combination of acts may in fact be less successful than one of the acts taken singly, there is no reason why this should not be represented in act-outcome expectancies. Hence, if an organism has the expectancies $a_1 a_2 Eo_1$ and $a_3 a_2 Eo_1$, it does not follow that it has the expectancy $(a_1, a_3)a_2 Eo_1$, where (a_1, a_3) is the simultaneous performance of a_1 and a_3. In general, act-outcome expectancies involving complex acts cannot be predicted on *a priori* grounds merely from knowledge of the expectancies concerning the acts taken singly; neither can the expectancies for single acts be deduced merely from knowledge of expectancies concerning these acts in combination. This is not inconsistent with the transitivity of acts in act-outcome expectancies asserted in

(5.3); the principle that $aa'Eo$ and $a'a''Eo$ imply $aa''Eo$ is silent concerning *combinations* of a, a', and a''.

Note that these comments apply only to cases in which two or more acts, each of which is intentional, have the same intended outcome. They are not concerned with cases in which two or more intentional acts directed toward different intended outcomes occur at the same time, such as, for instance, talking to someone to give him information and arranging the vocal and facial expression so as to indicate a friendly attitude. Nor do they apply to the simultaneous occurrence of intentional and nonintentional acts, such as talking and breathing.

Complex Intended Outcomes

A single act may have more than one expected outcome and, if it does, the outcomes will not in general have the same preference value for the subject—the components of a complex expected outcome may vary over a wide range from highly desired to highly aversive. Furthermore, what is objectively the same outcome may affect an organism's behavior toward it very differently according to its anticipated distance in time, space, and other variables; there is evidence for the existence of gradients of desiredness and aversiveness along such dimensions under a wide variety of conditions, in both human beings and animals.[1] As a single example, Renner (1966) found that rats tended, after experience in the situation, to choose the complex outcome of immediate shock followed by food over that of the same shock-food combination preceded by a 30-second delay. The reader is warned, however, that much of the work on gradients is open to interpretation in other than motivational terms.

Much effort has been invested in theoretical and experimental studies of the ways in which an organism arrives at a preference between two differential outcomes of which one or both are complex. This work has frequently aimed at the discovery of a utility function such that knowledge of the utility of each of the components of a complex outcome would permit calculation of the utility of the complex outcome itself. (For reviews, see Edwards, 1954 and 1961; Luce and Suppes, 1965.) "Utility" in this context closely resembles what is here called preference value, but it would be hazardous to identify the two concepts.

Three difficulties in developing strong measurement of utility may be mentioned here. First, as would be expected from SAO theory, there is a serious problem of disentangling the contributions of preferences and expectancies to a choice in cases in which the components of a complex outcome are probabilistic ("decision-making under uncertainty"); hence, parallel to the concept of utility there has developed the concept of "subjective probability," which obviously resembles (but, again, may not be identical with) the SAO notion of strength of expectancy. Secondly, the preference values or utilities of some outcomes are not independent of those of others. One shoe is of little value without the other member of the pair; a male without a female has no use for reproductive purposes; and, for different reasons, a cocktail may taste better if it contains bitters, even though the taste of bitters by themselves is aversive; an integral aspect of western music is the effective use of dissonant harmonies that are aversive standing alone or unresolved; and, departing from the perceptual level, the phenomena of "level of aspiration" (Lewin *et al.*, 1944) exist only because human beings are found to choose aversively difficult tasks. The similarity of this second point to what was said above about complex acts may be noted. The transitivity of preference (Formula 4.3) is not violated by such cases, since it says nothing about the relation of complex outcomes to their components. Thirdly, there may be an interaction between the preference value of a probabilistic outcome and the expectancy of the occurrence of the outcome. Within the admittedly small range of events that have been studied experimentally, both children (Marks, 1951) and college students (*e.g.*, Irwin and Snodgrass, 1966) tend to behave as if a preferred event were more probable than a dispreferred event when the objective probabilities of the two events are equal. The difficulties that would be created for decision theory by such an interaction have been discussed by Edwards (1962).

Decision Theory

SAO theory makes no advance commitment to any particular theory of the relation between the expectancies concerning complex acts and the expectancies concerning their components or of the relation between the preference value of complex outcomes and the preference values of their components. SAO theory does assert, however, that every choice involves an interlocked preference and pair of complementary act-outcome expectancies, the empirical criteria of which have been set forth in the preceding chapters, and only such theories as can be stated in these terms are relevant to it. A distinguishing feature of SAO theory is the fact that particular preferences and expectancies are diagnosable independently, whereas this is not true of utility and subjective probability in some important decision theories, notably, SEU theory.

Psychological Hedonism

SAO theory is not an instance of psychological hedonism, *i.e.*, it does not assert or imply that behavior is to be explained as directed toward pleasure and away from pain. In SAO theory, nonintentional behavior has no intended outcomes and is not *psychologically* directed toward anything; as for intentional acts, their intended outcomes are always the preferred members of the pairs of outcomes between which choices are made, but this is a tautologous assertion, deriving from definition, not from fact. Nothing in SAO theory excludes from behavior the extremes of heroism, martyrdom, altruism, egotism, or viciousness. Thus, it is a question of fact whether a given individual at a given time chooses an outcome that he believes will be beneficial to himself over one that he believes will be beneficial to someone else, or the other way around, granted that "beneficial" is defined by criteria other than the choice itself.[2]

CHOICE AND THE FLOW OF BEHAVIOR

In studying choices, it is convenient to arrange circumstances that are marked by definite decision-points such that the most prominent features of the situation, acts, and outcomes are experimentally well-defined and the observer knows that a choice has occurred and that it occurred at a particular time. Most of the examples in this book have been of this kind. Under conditions of naturalistic observation, however, although animals and human beings can sometimes be seen to arrive at choice-points, to deliberate, and to choose, behavior often seems to run more or less continuously for considerable lengths of time, even if the continuity is more like that of the flow of a shallow brook in a crooked and stony bed than that of a quiet river in a straight stretch. During such a period the observer would be unable to count with assurance the number of choices that the subject had made, or even perhaps to ascertain whether any choices had taken place at all. The remark that "All behavior can be said to involve deciding what to do and then doing it" (Poulton, 1966, p. 362) is not easy to apply to cases like these. Experimental work itself is not lacking in examples. The study of Skinnerian "free operant" bar-pressing by rats and key-pecking by pigeons typically eventuates in records an hour or more in length that are no more clearly punctuated by choices than are naturally occurring sequences of behavior of the same length; this accounts for the small use we have made of such information here.[3]

How smooth the surface of the moon looks depends upon the distance from which it is viewed and the power of the telescope that is brought to the eye's assistance. In the case of behavior, a dictionary sums up Samuel Johnson's seventy-five years by telling us that he was an English author and lexicographer; Boswell, however, carries us not only from year to year but sometimes from day to day and not infrequently reports the very words the great man used to put a conversational opponent in his place. An intelligence-test score or a statement of the number of seconds it took a rat to run a complex maze resembles the dictionary rather than Boswell. Both have their uses, but it is important that the scale of observation be adjusted to the scale of the question that is asked.

It is evident that much behavior is built hierarchically with goals, subgoals, and sub-subgoals, and that choices among alternatives are possible at each level. Deciding to write a string quartet and then doing it can be thought of as one choice and one act, but this act may extend over months of time and will be accomplished only by way of numerous acts of smaller scope, some of which are chosen only after agonizing consideration. At the same time, it is obvious that analysis can be carried too far, if one is interested in the composition as formed by decisions. It would be possible to count the number of notes in the final score; but, if this number turned out to be 25,000, it would be naive to suppose that writing them down was the result of 25,000 choices. The form of the composition exerts constraints upon the structure of the themes, the harmonies and their progressions, and the structure of such structures; and further constraints will be audible as exhibiting the composer's personal style and the style of his period. Some notes will follow others with no more call upon a decision-process than the reader needs if, when arising in the morning, he routinely puts on first his left shoe and then the right.

The phenomena of "tracking" behavior throw some light on the problem. Consider a subject who is confronted by the passage of a wavy line across the field of a small window and whose task is to keep a stylus or pointer as nearly as possible on the line, whether directly by hand or indirectly through the mediation of instruments. The subject may have undertaken the task to earn a fee, to forward the progress of science, or to do a favor to his instructor; but once he is engaged in the task, he has the highly specialized objective of keeping the pointer near the line, with his error continuously visible as a discrepancy between the two. Under such conditions, a subject does not respond to every visible discrepancy nor to every visible change in the size of the discrepancy, but only to those that fall outside some range of tolerance. Similarly, in studies of level of aspiration, where repeated performance involves discrete trials, each of which is scored according to some scale, the goal set by a subject on any trial is not, in general, the highest score theoretically possible in the task, but rather some level of performance within or near the range that his previous performances have shown to be possible for him. These momentary goals do not fluctuate with every vicissitude of his performance, but often stay fixed over a number of varying performances; and if the subject finally gives up in disgust, it is not because he has failed to approach or attain the maximum possible score, but because he has not been able to achieve some level set by himself as minimally satisfactory.

In neither tracking nor level of aspiration would it be sensible to count every period in which the pointer is not adjusted or the aspiration is not altered as a decision to accept the discrepancy that exists at the time. Nor, on the other hand, is it correct to regard each adjustment of the pointer or change in aspiration as the sign of a choice; to see this, it is sufficient to watch a driver's movements of the steering wheel of an automobile, most of which in a skilled operator are as automatic as the postural adjustments one makes in walking on a rough road.

In all of these cases, the question whether or not a particular act was or was not the result of a decision reduces, in SAO theory, to the question whether its occurrence depended upon an appropriate interlocked triad. The experimental tests in our present state of knowledge are likely to demand ingenuity and patience; they must be designed to determine whether the act in question varies with the subject's preferences and act-outcome expectancies as required by the definition of intentional acts. The principal difficulty of designing such tests would probably be to find ways of changing the preference and expectancies without altering the original task so greatly as to prevent the conclusions from being applicable to it.

AN ALTERNATIVE DIAGNOSTIC EXPERIMENT

The intimate relations among the criteria of discrimination, preference, and act-outcome expectancy suggest that it may be possible to collapse the standard discrimination-preference experiment and the standard act-outcome experiment into a single procedure that is diagnostic of all three states. An organism that managed to give positive results in such an experiment would be said to have exhibited intentional behavior. Such an experiment is schematized abstractly in Table 11.1.

In contrast to all of the illustrations in the previous chapters, Table 11.1 indicates that there are to be *four* different concurrent conditions and that the organism is to be exposed to all of these conditions in a single random order over trials. Presumably the series would contain the same

Table 11.1
Single standard experiment for diagnosing
discrimination, preference, and act-
outcome expectancy

	Conditions			
	x		x'	
	y	y'	y	y'
	1	2	3	4
a	+ o	− o	− o'	+ o'
a'	− o'	+ o'	+ o	− o

Note: x and x' are values of some experimental
variable and y and y' are values of some other experimental variable; a and a' are alternative acts; o and o'
are differential outcomes. *All four* conditions, 1, 2, 3,
4, are presented in a single random order.

number of trials of each condition. We then let x and x' be two values of
some experimental variable and y and y' those of another variable. Two
acts, a and a', are observed as usual, and two differential outcomes, o and
o', are provided.

If the organism being tested gives reliable results in the form indicated by the plus and minus signs of the table, the following assertions
would be consistent with the results:

1. The organism has behaved toward x and x' as if they were
discriminanda between which it discriminated, *i.e.*, as if xDx'. Note that
Conditions 1 and 3 constitute half of a standard discrimination experiment that happens to have been carried out in the presence of y, and that

Conditions 2 and 4 also constitute half of such an experiment carried out in the presence of y'.

2. The organism has behaved toward y and y' as if they were variables that varied its preference states in such a way that it preferred o to o', i.e., oPo', in conditions involving y and preferred o' to o, i.e., $o'Po$, in conditions involving y'. Thus, Conditions 1 and 3 constitute half of a standard preference experiment carried out in y-conditions and Conditions 2 and 4 constitute half of an identical experiment carried out in y'-conditions. The results are what would be expected if changing between y and y' reversed the organism's preference with respect to o and o'.

3. If oPo' in the presence of y and $o'Po$ in the presence of y', then Conditions 1 and 2 constitute half of a standard act-outcome experiment and the organism has behaved as if $aa'Eo$ and $a'aEo'$. Similarly, Conditions 3 and 4 constitute half of a standard act-outcome experiment in which the organism behaved as if $aa'Eo'$ and $a'aEo$.

What prevents us from concluding immediately that the organism did in fact display the discrimination, preferences, and act-outcome expectancies with which the results are consistent is the fact that the experiment did not provide an unconfounded reversal of the type required for a complete discrimination-preference experiment or of the type required for a complete act-outcome expectancy experiment. It will be recalled however, that these reversals had the function in each case of eliminating the possibility that the organism was displaying differential responses and biases but not discrimination and preference. The present experiment taken as a whole appears to handle this problem; no single differential response or bias associated with x, x', y, or y' is compatible with the results in the table, as the reader can see by testing the various conditions in pairs. One can, of course, consider the possibility that there are differential biases associated with pairs such as x and y, x and y', etc., and of testing for these biases by another four-condition experiment like that of Table 11.1 with the outcomes reversed in each column. It does not seem dangerous to put this aside as unnecessary or, at most, as a last resort under unusual circumstances.

Whether this new procedure should be substituted for the separate standard experiments of Chapters 3 and 5 is questionable. In the abstract, it has economy in its favor, and also whatever merit lies in the exhibition, in a single table of results, of interlocked preferences and act-outcome expectancies and their relation to discrimination. On the other side, however, is the fact that, as far as the writer knows, no such experiment has ever been performed, and it is not clear whether it would require too high an order of capacity on the part of an organism or an uneconomical expenditure of effort on the part of an experimenter to obtain positive results with unintelligent subjects or difficult experimental conditions. Furthermore, at the present time the writer can only invite the reader to consider what changes in the system of Part I would be necessitated if Table 11.1 were taken as the standard experiment for diagnosing discrimination, preference, and act-outcome expectancy.

SUMMARY

The terms "motivation" and "cognition" are not technical terms in SAO theory but may be used to refer, respectively, to preferences and to discriminations and expectancies. Motives of different degrees of generality exist, inasmuch as desires and aversions may be directed toward single individual objects or toward classes of objects whose preference values are intercorrelated over time or with variation of experimental conditions and that are to some degree mutually substitutable. Thus, a desire or aversion may be directed toward an individual person, as in love or hate, or toward a large inhomogeneous class of objects, as in a desire for food or an aversion to jazz music. In the case of general motives, the preference structure may be complex, as suggested by distinctions such as those between hunger and appetite and, in "achievement motivation," between desire for success and fear of failure. Intercorrelated classes of objects of preference and expectancy resemble concepts; in this sense, for example, a rat cannot be said to desire the death of a mouse without attributing to it the capacity to form this sort of concept of "dead mice."

Human beings sometimes form intentions toward intended outcomes that are known by the observer to be impossible. The observer's diagnosis of such intentions rests upon use of the diagnostic rules of Chapter 7 and of other principles, beyond the scope of the present work, including rules concerning generalization of expectancies and wagering behavior.

Intentional acts and intended outcomes may be complex; in such cases, the act-outcome expectancies concerning the complex acts and the preferences concerning the complex outcomes cannot be derived on *a priori* grounds from the expectancies and preferences concerning the component acts and outcomes. SAO theory requires some form of decision theory that employs the concepts of act-outcome expectancies and preferences, but makes no advance commitment to any one of the indefinitely large number of possible theories of this kind. SAO theory is not an instance of psychological hedonism.

From the point of view of SAO theory, much behavior is not intentional and therefore does not involve choices. In extended sequences of behavior that appears to flow freely, the question whether a particular act is or is not chosen reduces to the question whether it depends upon an appropriate interlocked triad; *i.e.*, whether it would vary if the act-outcome expectancies and preference were varied.

The standard discrimination-preference experiment and the standard act-outcome expectancy experiment can be collapsed into a single standard experiment from which all three states can be diagnosed, but the empirical and theoretical merits of substituting the single standard experiment for the other two are undecided at the present time.

NOTES AND COMMENTS

1. See, *e.g.*, Fajans, 1932; Hull, 1932; Miller, 1944; Irwin, Orchinik, and Weiss, 1946; Lambert and Solomon, 1952; Diggory, 1966; Renner, 1967; Irwin and Tolkmitt, 1968; Mischel, Grusec, and Masters, 1969.

2. It has probably become obvious to the reader that outcomes classified as desired and aversive by the definitions given here are not necessarily "pleasant" and "unpleasant," respectively, and that our affective scale is not a "hedonic" continuum. There are circumstances under which a bitter medicine or even pain itself may be strongly desired, and it is not only the puritan to whom various pleasures are abhorrent. Without attempting to argue it here, the suggestion is made that pleasant and unpleasant objects or states are those the desiredness or aversiveness of which is intrinsic; that is, the desiredness or aversiveness is not attributable to some other simultaneous or more remote outcome. The writer sees no way of avoiding a negative characterization of this sort while maintaining connection with empirical criteria.

3. The question whether a given act involves a single decision or some unknown number of decisions arises in an interesting way even in the case of rats running in a runway from a starting box to a goalbox. Logan (1966) performed an experiment in which rats received in the goalbox of such an apparatus a number of pellets of food that was negatively correlated with their running-speed, *i.e.*, they received a smaller reward the faster they ran. In one condition, for example, they received 1 pellet for running-times under 1½ sec., 2 pellets for times between 1½ and 2½ sec., 3 pellets for times between 2½ and 3½ sec., and so on. (The times were measured over a 6-ft. length of the 8-ft. alley.) It was found that the modal speed adopted by the rats when they obtained one pellet for each second of time in the alley was such as to give them three pellets; under conditions in which they obtained one pellet for each two seconds in the alley, they received a modal number of two pellets.

On various grounds of theory and experiment, Logan concluded that the animals did not make a single decision at the beginning of each run as to how fast to run on that trial, but rather monitored their speed continuously during the run, ". . . deciding at each moment whether to speed up or slow down" (Logan, 1966, p. 32). If this notion of continuous decision-making is to be taken literally, it would eliminate questions concerning the number of choices made by the subjects in the course of a run; but at the same time, it would come perilously close to eliminating also the very conception of choice itself. One supposes that the behavior, like that in tracking experiments, can be understood as governed by choices made when some tolerable discrepancy between position in the runway and time consumed (or anticipated time to the goalbox) is exceeded.

12

Quantitative Properties of Acts; Emotional States

In SAO theory the assertion that Act a is intentional, Ia, or that it is not intentional, $\sim Ia$, is a statement about a particular act that occurs at a particular time. A child opens a blue box; a rat turns to the right in a T-maze; each of these acts occurs at some dated moment in time and is either intentional or nonintentional, although of course we may not know which it is. In the tables and illustrations of the foregoing chapters, it has always been presumed that the observer was able to say whether or not an act had occurred; then, given that it occurred, the question of its intentionality could be raised.

At the same time, in order to determine whether or not an act was intentional, one needs to know whether or not its occurrence depended upon some interlocked triad; and to say that it did so is to claim that acts of its kind do not occur, under the prevailing conditions, if any of the members of the triad are absent. To establish this, we are driven to experiments in which we observe whether instances of the same kind of act occur when the preference and act-outcome expectancies are altered or are absent. Hence, in the illustrative tables, such a row designation as "a_1" or "turns right" has to be thought of as the name of a *class* of acts, and a plus or minus sign in a cell represents an observed number or relative frequency of occurrences of members of that class in a series of observations. Nevertheless, the final conclusion that Act a_1 (opening the blue box, or turning right) was or was not intentional applies to individual occurrences of these acts, even if the evidence comes from observations of other acts of the same kind under various conditions. "The same kind" means, of course, membership in the class defined in advance as a_1 or opening the blue box or turning right; it implies nothing about the intentionality of members of the class, not even that all members have the same status in this respect.

To base a systematic psychology upon binary choices in this way, rather than upon the easily obtained numerical values of latencies, rates, amplitudes, amounts (*e.g.*, of food or water) consumed, and other quantitative properties of acts may appear to run quite against the grain of progress. It is clear that a large part of the most sophisticated and technically advanced work in psychology at the present time centers upon just such quantitative data. Furthermore, it is not hard to find psychologists who claim that their fundamental interest lies in such data, which, for them, constitute the subject-matter of psychology; they look upon choices as secondary phenomena, derivable from laws of the "response-strengths" of competing acts.

Certainly, a major obstacle to the unification of psychological theory would be overcome if the relations between choices and the quantitative properties of the acts to be chosen between were understood; but this is far from being so. A good deal of theory and careful experimenting is going to be needed to bridge the gap between choices and measurable properties of the alternative acts taken singly and to indicate where, if anywhere, this cannot in principle be done. What follows attempts, not to solve this problem, but to provide a systematic context against which such attempts might be less fragmentary than they now tend to be. It will rest upon the distinction between cases in which the quantitative properties of an act are chosen by the organism and cases in which they are not chosen.[1]

CHOSEN QUANTITATIVE PROPERTIES OF ACTS

Whether or not an intentional act is successful in obtaining its intended outcome frequently, perhaps always, depends upon its latency, rate, amplitude, and the like. To catch a train, one may have to walk faster than usual; to be heard in a large auditorium, one's voice must be made louder; catching a fly requires a very speedy action of the hand. But success is not always positively related to the physical parameters of acts; the contingencies can be negative as well. A whisper may sometimes gain attention better than a shout, and the effect intended by a pianist may demand the lightest touch that is compatible with producing a tone at all. Such negative contingencies have recently been the subject of considerable attention in animal experiments, as witnessed by the frequent use of DRL ("differential reinforcement of low response rate") schedules of reward and the work of Logan (1966), discussed in the previous chapter, in which rats received fewer food pellets the faster they ran in an alley. In still other cases, there may be an optimal value or range of the parameter, on either side of which success is less likely. If it is valuable to be punctual, it may be well to be neither too early nor too late; to hit a target, one must aim neither too high nor too low and neither too much to the right or to the left.

There is little doubt that organisms are sensitive to these various contingencies, as Logan (1956, 1960) has maintained, and that they are able to choose, not merely to perform an act, but to perform it within some range of a scale of a significant quantitative property. Much of what is known as "skill" reflects delicate adjustments of such properties of acts. At the same time, the mere fact that an organism performs an act with a certain latency, force, or speed does not mean, of course, that that latency, force, or speed was chosen, even if the act itself was intentional. A mature organism has at its disposal a large repertoire of acts that have developed through automatized learning or maturation or both, the quantitative properties of which are characteristic of the individual and are likely to be subject to choice only on those infrequent special occasions when their normal levels are seen to be inadequate, as when one speaks particularly softly to avoid being overheard or particularly loudly in order to be heard at a distance. The likelihood that a speaker will have to be reminded to keep his voice down or to speak louder is a measure of his bias toward a characteristic level of loudness. Let the reader consider the difficulty he experiences in these cases, or in departing significantly from his accustomed rate of talking, walking, writing, and the like. It must not, of course, be supposed that an individual has just one characteristic loudness of voice or rate of walking; clearly, part of the process of automatization involves adjustments to a whole range of circumstances, so that, for example, one grades the loudness of his speech according to the distance of the auditor at least within certain limits of distance without the necessity of choosing to do so. A practiced public speaker may be expected to be adept at this sort of thing.

NONINTENTIONAL QUANTITATIVE PROPERTIES OF ACTS

It may seem to the reader that intentional acts and, perhaps especially, the desires and aversions upon which they depend, have been defined too bloodlessly. Aside from the fact that desires and aversions are preferences relative to ω and may be relatively strong or weak, may they not also be described as ardent, cool, superficial, profound, and the like? May not an act, however deliberate, be performed coldly or passionately, whether it be making a cutting remark, proposing marriage, or passing judgment on a convicted criminal?

It is true that the results of a standard preference experiment can tell us whether a rat or a human being desired food or a female or was averse to electric shock or to public humiliation, but do not tell us whether these desires and aversions were ardent, profound, or passionate. Nevertheless, an observer who watched the behavior of the subject in such an experiment might arrive at opinions on questions like this, and unless these opinions are scientifically worthless, they must have been based upon aspects of the behavior that are not captured by the choices tabulated from the standard experiment. Uninspiring as much of the history of discussions about the relations between motivation and emotion may be, it is hard to put these problems aside without at least an attempt to clarify them. If the language of emotions were restricted to poetry, fiction, and common speech and were notably absent from sober reports in psychological journals, perhaps one could dismiss the questions as somehow esthetic or wholly misconceived, but this is far from true. Although some psychologists have abandoned the concept, or at least the word, "emotion," others use it freely, even if they are ill at ease about its relation to motivation, its distinguishing features, and its theoretical status in general.

It will have been observed that, in introducing the topic, we have spoken of both preference states and acts as possibly being emotional. Since preferences and acts are quite different sorts of things, it seems likely that the concept of emotion is being used differently when applied to these two cases. Let us consider first what kind of evidence leads to an act's being called emotional.

EMOTIONAL ACTS

Imagine two friends in a discussion that becomes more and more heated. What is the evidence of the "heat"? Clearly, having a discussion is not itself necessarily emotional, nor are the acts of uttering sentences that are intended to state facts, derive conclusions, and convince or persuade. But if the voices are raised, so that they become louder in volume and higher in pitch; if the faces become red; if the gestures increase in amplitude and are participated in by more parts of the body; and if words are used that violate the conventions of friendly and courteous exchange —then one sees that the behavior has become emotional.

Now all of these phenomena are capable of being interpreted as what we have called nonintentional biases. They are acts, or properties of acts, that appear not to be directed toward intended outcomes, although they may indeed have important and, perhaps, undesired outcomes. The two persons may still be cool enough to know this but too heated for this knowledge to prevent the impending catastrophe. The tone of voice, the circulatory changes, the overemphatic gestures, and the use of language in disregard of its probable consequences are recognized as biases by the observer who describes the behavior of the disputants as having gotten "out of control."

Notice that the observer's diagnosis is analytic, not merely descriptive; that is, it asserts something about the psychological status of the behavior. This can easily be seen from the fact that the same observer seeing exactly the same behavior (except possibly for the red faces) of the same persons when they were acting parts on a stage, would regard the behavior as skillfully intentional and "controlled." On the stage, the acts would be perceived as directed toward the intended outcome of a good simulation of emotional behavior, that is, of a kind of behavior that, off the stage, is nonintentional.

If we accept this line of thought, it means that at least some acts can be emotional under one set of conditions and nonemotional under another; that is, knowledge about the act itself is not sufficient to put it into one of these two classes. Looking at the same illustration, and considering the criteria of intentional acts, we suppose that the observer of the dispute on the stage diagnoses the behavior as intentional, and nonemotional, in the belief that if the preference states and act-outcome expectancies of the actors were suddenly altered, the behavior would change accordingly. Thus, if the action was taking place in the rehearsal of a play, and the director interrupted it with instructions to change it from excited passion to cold controversy, the actors' skill and control would be shown by their playing the scene immediately in this altogether different way. If the director said, "Instead of making your voices louder and higher, try playing it softer and lower," they would no doubt be able to comply. But if the dispute was genuine and the emotions of the participants were highly aroused, no such ready and appropriate modification to the requirements of a new preference state or new expectancies would be anticipated. It is just such resistance to intentional control that would lead us to classify the resisting acts, or properties of them, as biases.

Two points need to be added, however. First, if the director asked the players to make their faces redder, or to make them white instead of red, they might correctly claim an inability to do this. Or, being asked to shed tears, one actor might do so without external aid (onion juice?) and another not. Human beings differ with respect to their intentional control over some acts, and still other acts are never under such control (unless, perhaps, in a psychological laboratory). Yet these acts are typically regarded as signs of emotion and, because many of them are functions of the autonomic nervous system, some psychologists have gone so far as to identify emotions with autonomic activities. It can be seen that no such identification is made here. In this connection, if an actor claims that he enters an emotional state when he plays an emotional scene, we would of course take this to mean that some of his acts, or properties of them, are not under his intentional control; were he to deny this, he would either be mistaken about his own state or would be disagreeing with the conception of emotion being developed here.[2,3]

Secondly, questions of *degree* of intentional control arise. Even under intensely emotional conditions, an important change in the situation may lead to an immediate modification of the behavior. Upon the appearance of someone who should not see them quarreling, the two parties to a dispute might lower their voices, restrain their gestures, and moderate their language; they might even be able to pretend that all was as usual, and engage in neutral conversation with the third person. It is clear that this is not an all-or-none matter. The voices might be softened and the gestures reduced but not to a level that would hide the emotion from the new observer; or the changes might go too far, so that the observer would notice the abnormally quiet and rigid aspect they presented. The changes to new levels of voice and gesture would be intentional, if they depended, say, upon a desire to conceal the quarrel and upon the act-outcome expectancies that this outcome was more likely with lowered voices and normal gestures than without such changes and that discovery was more likely in the converse case. The failure to achieve normal levels would simultaneously signify the existence of biases characteristic of an emotional state.

EMOTIONS AS "MOTIVES" OF INTENTIONAL BEHAVIOR

It was suggested above that both acts and preference states may be called emotional, and that this reflects two different functions of the term. Thus far, the discussion has centered upon emotional states as factors that bias the quantitative properties of acts; now they must be considered in their role as "motivators" of intentional behavior. The distinction can be seen in the dispute that has been used as an illustration, where the emotionality of the behavior was judged by the tones of voice, amplitude of gesture, and the like. Suppose that in addition to this, one of the disputants makes slighting references to the other's intelligence or honesty and does this with the intention of injuring him; the observer may conclude that these intentional acts were motivated by anger and would not otherwise have occurred, and the offending party may later, in a cooler moment, agree with this. The question is, what can it mean to assert that an intentional act is motivated by an emotion?

There are at least three possible answers to this question along the lines of the present discussion. First, an emotional state may facilitate or inhibit an intentional act. Secondly, if an emotional state itself is desirable or aversive, an organism may behave with the intention of producing it, eliminating it, or increasing or decreasing its intensity. Thirdly, an emotional state may create, abolish, strengthen, or weaken desires and aversions for objects other than the state itself. Each of these possibilities will be discussed in turn.

Inhibition and Facilitation of Intentional Acts; "Impulsive" Acts

The biasing effects of emotional states are not limited to such quantitative properties of acts as their latencies and amplitudes, but may go so far as to determine whether or not an act occurs at all. This is true of both intentional and nonintentional acts.

In intentional behavior, either or both of the alternative acts may be facilitated or inhibited by the biasing state. A person who finds that his intended act is overridden by a bias, so that he performs its alternative or some other act, may complain or apologize for what he has done on the grounds that he didn't "mean" to do it and that he is as surprised as the observer. If the nonintentional act happens to have an unexpectedly gratifying outcome, he confronts the minor ethical dilemma between accepting undeserved credit for the result and disavowing it.

On the other hand, if an intended act is facilitated by a biasing state, so that it occurs more quickly or forcefully than would otherwise have been the case or even occurs when otherwise it would have failed to occur, it may be called "impulsive." Here, too, the person may have reason to wish to disavow the outcome and, if so, he might admit to a fleeting intention toward it that had somehow flowed over into action before he had reached an appropriate decision point. To knock someone down with a skillful blow or to injure his feelings with a shrewd comment is too obviously dependent upon the actor's personal history to be put aside as a reflexive or instinctive response to the situation and therefore as nonintentional. At the same time, such impulsive acts are likely to occur with unusually short latencies and to exhibit unconcern with remote differential outcomes. If such an act would not have taken place in the absence of the appropriate interlocked preference and act-outcome expectancies, it was by definition intentional. If it would not have occurred in the absence of a biasing emotional state, it was emotional. If both sets of determiners were required for its occurrence, it was both intentional and emotional.[4,5]

These distinctions among classes of acts have practical as well as theoretical implications, especially insofar as they bear upon questions of human beings' moral, ethical, and legal responsibility for their acts. But even if the distinctions themselves are conceptually clear, the reader who has appreciated the difficulty and subtlety of diagnosing states of preference and expectancy will not imagine that differential diagnosis can be accomplished easily and confidently. It will be hard to do even with the resources of laboratory experimentation and control; when unique individual instances of behavior are in question, as is the case when personal responsibility is to be judged, the state of the science is likely to be useful marginally, if at all. Still, the theoretician can hope that clarification of concepts will assist practical judgment even when action must be taken on the basis of very imperfect information.

A particularly difficult problem is presented by complex and well-directed acts that are performed under emergency conditions, seemingly without time for deliberation and evaluation of their possible consequences. Heroic interventions in which the actor attempts to save the life of another person with apparent disregard of his own safety are examples of this, particularly when the time-scale of the episode is very short and the action itself is one never before performed by the actor. Failing to give aid may occur under similar circumstances and is at least equally difficult to interpret as intentional or nonintentional. We are able only to suggest that some proportion of these acts are expressions of contingent intentions that may have been rehearsed far in advance of the emergency; one can imagine such situations or hear of their real occurrence, and can resolve to behave in such and such a way if ever confronted by a like emergency. The psychological problems that arise here are special cases of those referred to in Note 3, Chapter 6.

Emotions as Desired or Aversive

That emotions may be desired or aversive is one of the few assertions about them—perhaps the only one—that is never denied, although differences of terminology make one writer refer to their pleasantness and unpleasantness, another to their positive and negative hedonic tone, etc. Although the degree of desiredness and aversiveness is taken to be variable, the notion of a completely neutral emotion is, or comes close to being, a self-contradiction among psychologists who use the concept at all. Thus, Tolman (1932, p. 264) said that an emotion is ". . . first of all, a pleasantness or unpleasantness," and Hebb (1949) thought that a corresponding classification of dispositions, behaviorally defined, was possible and useful. Hull seems not to have used the word in his *Principles of behavior* (1943), but in *A behavior system* (1952, p. 355) he regarded the emotions as urgently needing to be incorporated into systematic psychology and referred to the work of Brown and Farber (1951) as "an excellent groundwork" for this. It is not surprising to find that Brown and Farber dealt particularly with the aversive state of frustration, rather than with a desired state; the latter would be much harder to treat as a state whose reduction in intensity would be "reinforcing" in the Hullian sense.

We accept the supposition that emotions may be desired or aversive but, except for precedent, there seems to be no reason to exclude the possibility that they may be neutral. This has already been foreshadowed in Chapter 10, as were also the suppositions that what is called the same emotion may, at different times or at different intensities, sometimes be desired, sometimes neutral, and sometimes aversive, and that these are questions of experimental fact, not of the definition of emotional states. Anyone who *defines* fear and anger as aversive will be puzzled, as some have been, by the desiredness of a fearsome roller-coaster ride or the voluptuous delight of righteous anger.

Given that emotional states may be desired or aversive (whatever else is true of them), behavior can be expected that has as its intended outcome the induction or increase in strength of a desired emotion and the abolition or reduction of an aversive one. If emotions are as frequent and as intensely desired and aversive as they are often thought to be, a correspondingly large amount of organisms' behavior will be both intentionally and habitually directed toward these outcomes.

Desires and Aversions Created by Emotional States

It is obvious that whatever is instrumental in bringing about desired emotional states or in eliminating aversive ones may acquire induced desirability; similarly, whatever is instrumental in eliminating desired states or inducing aversive ones may acquire induced aversiveness. If seeing a loved person after an interval of separation is an occasion for joy, means of bringing this about may be sought and hindrances to it may be avoided; if symptoms of illness create fear and fear is aversive, then whatever removes the fear (regardless of its effect upon the symptoms) may be desired, and whatever aggravates the fear may become aversive. These are special cases of the general problem of derived or acquired preference value and therefore subject to the same laws, whatever these may be.

Contemporary experimental psychology makes a great deal of use of the conception of emotions as aversive and of derived or "conditioned" aversiveness of originally neutral objects and situations due in one way or another to their association with aversive emotions (see, for example, Miller (1948); Solomon and Brush (1956); Rescorla and Solomon (1967); and other discussions of the two-process theory of avoidance learning). One might have thought in advance that desired emotions and derived desirability of originally neutral situations and objects would be treated like their aversive parallels, but the literature fails to exhibit this anticipated symmetry. Theories of acquired desirability (most commonly studied as "secondary reinforcement") have seldom postulated desired emotional states, a fact that clearly reflects the one-sidedness of the concept of "drive."

A relation between emotional states and desires and aversions compatible with that just discussed, but distinct from it, has come from students of animal behavior, especially the ethologists. According to this view, various emotions have associated with them, perhaps indeed as constituents of them, particular acts or sequences of acts called "consummatory." (The student is warned against being misled by taking this word as if it were derived from "to consume"; it comes from the Latin "to accomplish" or "to complete.") The final species-specific acts of eating, copulating, "threatening" in territorial defense, fighting, and the like are seen as manifestations of distinct emotional states and their natural culmination in behavior. It is possible that the very performance of such acts is desired and that this desiredness is innately determined rather than derived or learned. Tinbergen (1951, p. 106) remarks that "Even psychologists who have watched hundreds of rats running a maze rarely realize that, strictly speaking, it is not the litter or the food that the animal is striving towards, but the performance itself of the maternal activities or eating." Among psychologists who have *not* overlooked this may be numbered Sheffield, Roby, and Campbell (1954); they have argued that it is consummatory acts of ingestion, rather than reduction of hunger, that "reinforce" rats' speed of running in a runway.

Nothing in SAO theory prohibits the performance of an act from being desired or aversive; indeed this was brought forward as a possibility abstractly in Chapter 4, and concretely in Chapter 6 in the instances of mouse-killing by rats (Myer and White, 1965) and agonistic (threatening) behavior in Siamese fighting fish (Thompson, 1963). It is interesting that the question arises in connection with supposedly instinctive behavior; questions of innate or "instinctive" acts are hard to avoid when problems of emotion are at issue, as the history of both topics amply shows. (If documentation is needed, the names of James (1890) and McDougall (1923) will suffice.)

If an act is conceived of as desired or aversive, and thus as an object of preference, this means, of course, that it is being considered as a possible *outcome of some prior act*. For example, if the rats in Myer and White's experiment are said to have desired to kill mice, this is because the rats chose mouse-killing over ω as a differential outcome in a preference experiment; mouse-killing was the outcome of prior acts of turning right or turning left, as the case might be, in the T-maze. The fact that mouse-killing is desired does not tell us whether it is intentional or nonintentional; it could be either. It is the acts of turning right and turning left that are shown by the experiment to be intentional. Furthermore, when an act is treated as an outcome, there will always be a delicate problem of diagnosis of the effective outcome in the situation, since the act will itself have outcomes, if only the proprioceptive feedback from its performance. This difficulty can be seen in Sheffield, Roby, and Campbell's treatment of the act of ingestion as a "reinforcer." Their rats were ingesting sweet substances, and the question arises as to whether the object of desire was the act of ingestion or the taste of the sweet substance or both. The authors believed ". . . that sweet stimulation innately elicits ingestion and that this reinforces instrumental learning in proportion to the strength of the ingestion response" (Sheffield, Roby, and Campbell, 1954, p. 353), but other interpretations are possible. The beautiful experiments of Epstein and Teitelbaum (1962) showed that neither innately determined acts of ingestion nor sensations from food in the mouth are necessary for maintenance of body weight and good health in adult rats, which displayed a remarkable capacity to feed themselves by the unnatural means of pressing a bar that automatically gave them food through a gastric tube that bypassed the normal route of mouth and pharynx. These results should give pause to anyone who wishes to give consummatory acts a central place in a theory of behavior, but they should not discourage research on the intrinsic desiredness and aversiveness of acts that are characteristic of instincts and emotional states.

It must be pointed out that the notion of consummatory acts, whatever may be its usefulness when applied to infrahuman behavior, becomes very slippery when human beings are concerned. Returning for a moment to our example of a dispute, if one of the parties is sufficiently angered by what the other says and suddenly knocks him down, this act might be thought of as the consummatory act emanating from an aggressive emotional state, and this is indeed the way it is treated by Lorenz, an enormously knowledgable student of behavior in animals. Dealing with such a case in his book, *On aggression* (1969, p. 44), he supposes that what he himself would want under the circumstances would be to give his opponent a thorough beating, not for the satisfaction of hurting or killing him, but so as to demonstrate physical and mental superiority over him. One wonders whether Lorenz has permitted himself to imagine the state of someone who, powerless to intervene, must watch a woman being raped or a child being beaten to death, or the state of the holiday crowds that we are told have often massed to enjoy a public hanging and disembowelment. It is not easy to follow Lorenz's transition from this attitude to his handling, later in the same book, of the cruel history and even more threatening future of human violence. But this is a side-issue; even if self-analysis were a good way to answer such questions, it is evident that he is now defining consummatory acts functionally, as whatever acts assuage an emotional drive, rather than by the characteristics of the act itself. Making a cutting remark is then just as much a consummatory act as knocking one's enemy down, given that it equally discharges such a drive. So also is pressing the button that wipes out a whole enemy people. With all respect to Lorenz, one doubts the wisdom of stressing parallels, however striking, between the phenomena of aggression in human beings and those in baboons, wolves, and ravens.[6]

At the same time, the problem that Lorenz points to is vital. Human beings do often desire to inflict injury, pain, debasement, and even death to their fellows. It is also true that they often desire the growth, health, and happiness of their fellows. Anyone who believes that our present understanding of motivation and learning genuinely accounts for such phenomena is easily satisfied. In sympathy with Lorenz, the writer suspects that experimental psychologists are overoptimistic about the power of the psychology of learning and believes that the species-specific biological nature of man, as well as that of lower animals, will in the end play a larger role in the theory of emotion and motivation than it now does.

WHAT ARE EMOTIONS?

Although the principal aim of this book is to lay a firm basis for understanding intentional behavior and the psychological processes upon which it depends, we have been unable to escape the knotty problems associated with the idea of emotion. The discussion has assigned two roles to emotional states insofar as they are related to intentional acts, namely, that of biasing the quantitative properties of such acts, including facilitations and inhibitions of them, and that of creating, by one or another of several mechanisms, desired and aversive outcomes toward which intentional behavior may be directed; but no definition of the concept of emotion has been offered.

The writer's opinion is that the word "emotion," as was said above about "motivation," is useful when precision is either not desired or not attainable; again, like "motivation," it is not a technical term in an SAO system and will not be formally defined. It has been implicit in the discussion of emotional states that they are biasing dispositions, and that they may be desired or aversive or may be associated with, or responsible for, the desiredness or aversiveness of other outcomes; and it should be noted that the concepts of bias, desiredness, and aversiveness *are* technical terms and *are* defined in the present system. It is not clear that an attempt to distinguish sharply between emotional and nonemotional biases, desires, and aversions is worth the effort and would, even if successful, reflect a genuine psychological distinction rather than an arbitrary set of criteria drawn from such disparate considerations as those of neural and endocrine physiology, genetics, the topography of behavior, the psychology of learning, and mere convenience. The notion of a biasing disposition is always in the neighborhood when emotions are discussed; what seems to be important is not whether such a disposition is emotional but whether the behavior that one is trying to understand is subject to such and such a disposition and, if so, what concretely the relation happens to be.

The status of common-language names of emotions is at least as doubtful as that of the general term, "emotion," itself. The words, "anger," "rage," "frustration," and "aggression," refer to phenomena that are unquestionably important, not only in the psychology of the individual organism, but for large issues ranging from biological evolution to war and the future of human society. But the literature that deals seriously with these phenomena is by general acknowledgment almost incredibly confused and disheartening to a scientist, and will surely be so to a student who reads such a sample of it as, say, Dembo (1931), Dollard *et al.* (1939), Maier (1949), Amsel and Roussel (1952), Lorenz (1969), and Schachter and Singer (1962). What is discouraging is not the lack of interesting facts, of which there are many, but the theoretical disarray that permits one writer to build a structure out of just those facts that another sees as irrelevant. Attempts to refine the usage of words like "anger" and "frustration" so as to make acceptable technical terms of them seem hopeless; the same can be said of other words referring to so-called emotions, such as "fear" and "anxiety." Perhaps in the long run psychologists must resort to new words, or to technical symbols that are embedded in particular theories (*e.g.*, Brown and Farber's (1951) "*F*" and Amsel's (1958) $r_F - s_F$, which are theoretically distinct conceptions, although derived from considerations of "frustration."

RELATIONS TO OTHER CONCEPTIONS OF EMOTIONS

Competing conceptions of emotions are numerous and heterogeneous enough to dismay a student of psychology, as was said above. Surveys and reviews are not hard to find; Arnold's (1960) admirable history and analysis of the field is the best that is known to the writer. A few brief comments on the relations of some of the more familiar conceptions to those of SAO theory appear to be in order.

Emotions as Conscious Experiences

That emotions have often been thought of as particular kinds of "conscious experience" is sufficiently demonstrated by the James-Lange theory, which claimed that emotions were the subject's awareness of physiological and behavioral processes aroused by certain characteristic sorts of situations. The SAO view is that emotions are dispositions that are manifested as behavioral biases. Whether or not a subject is aware of such a state is a question of fact, as maintained in Chapter 8.

Emotions as Affects

It has been held that emotions are "an acutely disturbed affective state" (Young, 1961, p. 409). The SAO view is that emotional states may have any degree of desiredness or aversiveness and may even be neutral.

Emotions as Physiological Activities

Cannon's (1927) study of physiological processes in pain, hunger, fear, and rage encouraged some psychologists to identify emotions with such processes, especially with those controlled by the autonomic nervous system. SAO theory rejects this identification, but takes these processes as evidence of emotional states insofar as they are describable as biased acts.

Emotions and States of "Energy Mobilization," "Arousal," or "Activation"

Relations between quantitative properties of acts and emotions have been stressed by a number of psychologists (*e.g.*, Duffy (1951), Lindsley (1951), and Malmo (1959)), encouraged in recent years by the discovery of associations between level of excitation of the reticular formation and a physiological or behavioral dimension ranging from sleep to excitment. As has been seen, the SAO conception of emotion rests upon biases in quantitative properties of acts; and variations in "energy mobilization," "arousal," or "activation" would undoubtedly be reflected in these biases. It is necessary to point out, however, that emotional states as conceived in SAO theory may be either excited or depressed, depending upon the direction of the biases that are concerned.

Emotions and Drives

More than thirty years ago, Skinner (1938, p. 407) wrote of emotion as a state "comparable in many respects with a drive." It is interesting that usage, at least among American psychologists, has fairly consistently treated hunger and thirst as drives, but sex, fear, and frustration sometimes as drives and sometimes as emotions. It is hard to see what distinction is being relied upon, except that deprivation operations are useful for varying hunger and thirst, less so for sex, and seemingly irrelevant for fear and frustration. From the point of view of SAO theory, the concept of emotion is not required if hunger or thirst means only desire for food or water, and sex, desire for copulation, and fear or frustration, aversion to some object or situation. But if, aside from such desires or aversions, a state of "drive" is invoked, this implies intercorrelated changes in the quantitative properties of some set of acts. Some of these changes might be intentional; but those that are nonintentional would qualify as emotional biases, in our sense. Thus, whether "hunger" is or is not emotional depends upon whether it is simply a desire for food or whether it is a state that biases nonintentionally the quantitative properties of the organism's behavior.

Emotions as Disorganizing Influences

Some conceptions of emotion either define it as a state, psychological or physiological, that disrupts or disorganizes behavior or take such effects to be inevitable consequences of emotions (see, for example, discussions by Leeper (1948), Hebb (1949), and Arnold (1960)). The notion of disruption or disorganization of behavior can, of course, mean many different things. If one uses as a criterion of disruption the lowering of the probability that an intentional act will actually have its intended outcome, then it can be seen from the above discussion that such disruption is not a defining characteristic of emotional states in SAO theory; whether a particular emotional state reduces the likelihood that an intentional act will be successful is a question of fact, the answer to which depends upon the direction and strength of the emotional biases and the nature of the particular intentional act whose success is at issue. Emotional states can facilitate intentional acts, but they can also inhibit them or facilitate nonintentional acts that interfere with their performance.

SUMMARY

SAO definitions of intentional and nonintentional acts rest upon experimental observations of relative frequencies of subjects' performances of alternative acts in binary-choice situations, rather than upon observations of such quantitative properties of acts as their latencies, amplitudes, and rates. Psychological theory has not yet provided a unified set of principles that incorporate both kinds of data and the relations between them. It is argued here that, in some cases, quantitative properties of acts are chosen by the organism and therefore are included in the definition of the intentional acts themselves; but that in other cases, the quantitative properties of acts are not chosen and are therefore nonintentional, even if they are properties of acts that are themselves intentional.

Nonintentional quantitative properties of acts may appear in the form of biases, and "emotional states" can be regarded as dispositions that manifest themselves in such biases. Emotional states may "motivate" intentional acts in at least three ways: first, by facilitating or inhibiting such acts; second, by being themselves desired or aversive, and thus providing the required preferences of intentional acts; and third, by creating or being associated with desires and aversions for objects other than the emotional states themselves.

This conception of emotions is distinguished from those that regard them as conscious experiences, as affects, as physiological activities, as reflections of "energy mobilization," "arousal," or "activation," as "drives," and as disorganizing influences.

NOTES AND COMMENTS

1. On the relation between choices and the quantitative properties of acts see, for example, Renner (1964), Norman (1966), Shimp (1969), and Catlin and Gleitman (1968).

2. The question whether or not an actor on the stage actually enters the emotional state he intends to mimic has a parallel in human interactions whenever one person intentionally uses emotional expression as a means of influencing another. Goffman (1967, p. 23, footnote) gives the following example among many others:

> Even when a child demands something and is refused, he is likely to cry and sulk not as an irrational expression of frustration but as a ritual move, conveying that he already has a face to lose and that its loss is not to be permitted lightly. Sympathetic parents may even allow for such display, seeing in these crude strategies the beginnings of a social self.

In the present view, it is quite possible for the emotion to be genuine enough and yet to have been at least partially self-induced as a "ritual move." If a person learns how to bring about emotional states in himself, nothing prevents his doing so intentionally. Frequent use of this device is not without risk, since it puts the user at the mercy of the induced biasing effects and also provides opportunities for Pavlovian conditioning of the emotional state to irrelevant aspects of the situations and thereby reduces the scope of intentional control over the state.

3. Several investigators have recently reported instrumental learning of visceral and glandular acts that are commonly regarded as not subject to intentional control. For example, Miller and DiCara (1967) gave rats rewarding electrical brain stimulation when their heart rates increased in the presence of a discriminandum (a flashing light and a tone) but gave no reward in the presence of δ; over a series of trials, the animals' heart rates came to be more rapid in the rewarded than in the non-rewarded condition. Similar positive results were obtained in animals that were rewarded for a decrease, rather than an increase, in rate. This work and a considerable number of related experiments have been reviewed by Katkin and Murray (1968) and Miller (1969).

The phenomena are striking, but whether they amount to the subjects' gaining intentional control over visceral and glandular activities is still doubtful, in the present writer's opinion. To his knowledge, none of these experiments as yet fully meet the requirements of a standard discrimination-preference experiment (Chapter 3) or a standard act-outcome expectancy experiment (Chapter 5). In particular, the require-ment of trial-by-trial random order of discriminanda in the former case and opposed preference states in the latter case has not been met; and this may not be a trivial matter. Whatever the final result of these lines of research, they promise to throw new light on problems of classification of behavior and of its determinants.

4. The word "impulsive" seems to be applied commonly only to acts that have an intentional component. It would not be used, for example, for nonintentional belching in company nor for nonintentional raucous laughter at a speaker's embarrassing *faux pas*, even though the act is prohibited by rules of etiquette and in the latter case depends upon the laugher's perception and evaluation of what the speaker said and therefore upon the laugher's cultural history.

5. Because an act may have both intentional and biased properties at the same time, the alternative acts in experiments on choice behavior need to be as unsusceptible to bias as possible or, failing this, as nearly as possible equally susceptible. Counterbalancing procedures are, of course, frequently used to eliminate bias from the overall results. From this point of view, it is probably better to require a human subject to press one of two keys or buttons than to have him utter words such as "yes" and "no" or "heavier" and "lighter." The significance of the arbitrary acts of pressing keys or buttons can readily be reversed, but the same could not be said of a procedure in which counterbalancing required a subject to say "heavier" when he means "lighter" or "yes" when he means "no."

It is very common to require both human and animal subjects to choose between performing some act, *a*, and abstaining from Act *a*. Although such pairs of alternatives are extremely convenient, it is easy to see that they are not optimal selections on an experimenter's part if Act *a* is subject to biases, emotional or otherwise. The question needs study, but it seems unlikely that Act *a* and abstaining from Act *a* will generally be facilitated and inhibited by the same conditions; one might expect condi-tions that facilitated *a* to make it more difficult to abstain from *a*, and conditions that inhibited *a* to make it easier to abstain from *a*.

6. Premack (1965 and elsewhere) has developed the hypothesis that the more probable of two responses will "reinforce" the less probable. Some of the force of this hypothesis derives from his demonstrations that animals can use supposedly consummatory acts instrumentally; for ex-ample, a rat can be trained not only to run in order to drink, but also to drink in order to run. Such demonstrations appear to throw doubt on the special properties of the "consummatory" acts that can be so manipu-lated. A full treatment of the relation between Premack's conception of

reinforcement and the SAO conception of preference cannot be offered here. It can only be suggested that if a "less probable" act (say, a) is directed toward the performance of a "more probable" act (say, a'), then a is a chosen act whose intended outcome is a' or some consequence of a'. If the performance of a were more probable than that of a', it would often be the case that the organism would prefer to continue performing a rather than proceeding to a'. It is not obvious that critical cases can be found in which a' "reinforces" a even though a' or its consequences are not preferred to a or its consequences.

References

Amsel, A. The role of frustrative nonreward in noncontinuous reward situations. *Psychol. Bull.*, 1958, 55, 102-119.

Amsel, A., and Roussel, J. Motivational properties of frustration: I. Effect on a running response of the addition of frustration to the motivational complex. *J. exp. Psychol.*, 1952, 43, 363-368.

Anscombe, G. E. M. *Intention*. Ithaca, N.Y.: Cornell Univ. Press, 1966.

Arnold, M. B. *Emotion and personality*. (2 vols.) N.Y.: Columbia Univ. Press, 1960.

Arrow, K. J. *Social choice and individual values*. N.Y.: Wiley, 1951.

Atkinson, J. W. (Ed.) *Motives in fantasy, action, and society*. N.Y.: Van Nostrand, 1958.

Ball, G. G. Separation of electrical self-stimulation and electrically elicited eating in the hypothalamus. *Communications in behavioral Biol.*, 1969, 3, 5-10.

Bentham, J. *An introduction to the principles of morals and legislation*. N.Y.: Hafner Publ. Co., 1948. (First publication 1789)

Besch, N. F., Morris, H., and Levine, S. A comparison between correction and noncorrection methods in drive discrimination. *J. exp. Psychol.*, 1963, 65, 414-419.

Birenbaum, G. Das Vergessen einer Vornahme. *Psychol. Forsch.*, 1930, 13, 218-284.

Birney, R. C., Burdick, H., and Teevan, R. C. *Fear of failure*. N.Y.: Van Nostrand-Reinhold, 1969.

Bolles, R. C. The usefulness of the drive concept. In: M. R. Jones (Ed.), *Nebraska symposium on motivation*. Lincoln, Nebr.: Nebraska Univ. Press, 1958, pp. 1-33.

Bolles, R. C. A psychophysical study of hunger in the rat. *J. exp. Psychol.*, 1962, 63, 387-390.

Bolles, R. C. *Theory of motivation*. N.Y.: Harper and Row, 1967.

Bolles, R., and Petrinovich, L. A technique for obtaining rapid drive discrimination in the rat. *J. comp. physiol. Psychol.*, 1954, 47, 378-380.

Brown, J. S., and Farber, I. E. Emotions conceptualized as intervening variables—with suggestions toward a theory of frustration. *Psychol. Bull.*, 1951, 48, 465-495.

Brown, R. *Social psychology*. N.Y.: Free Press, 1965.

Brunswik, E. Probability as a determiner of rat behavior. *J. exp. Psychol.*, 1939, 25, 175-197.

Campbell, B. A., and Misanin, J. R. Basic drives. *Annu. Rev. Psychol.*, 1969, 20, 57-84.

Cannon, W. B. *Bodily changes in pain, hunger, fear and rage.* N.Y.: D. Appleton, 1927.

Cannon, W. B. Hunger and thirst. In: C. Murchison (Ed.), *Handbook of general experimental psychology.* Worcester, Mass.: Clark Univ. Press, 1934, pp. 247-263.

Catlin, J., and Gleitman, H. Relations between choice and latency measures in a selective learning paradigm. *J. math. Psychol.*, 1968, 5, 422-441.

Cheng, Fa-Yu. Drive discrimination learning under conflict conditions. *Acta psychologica Taiwanica*, 1960, No. 2 [no Vol. No.], 7-32.

Cofer, C. N., and Appley, M. H. *Motivation: theory and research.* N.Y.: Wiley, 1964.

Coombs, C. H., Dawes, R. M., and Tversky, A. *Mathematical psychology. An elementary introduction.* Englewood Cliffs, N.J.: Prentice-Hall, 1970.

Coons, E. E., Levak, M., and Miller, N. E. Lateral hypothalamus: learning of food-seeking response activated by electrical stimulation. *Science*, 1965, 150, 1320-1321.

Cowles, J. T. Food-tokens as incentives for learning by chimpanzees. *Comp. Psychol. Monogr.*, 1937, 14, No. 5.

Dembo, T. Der Aerger als dynamisches Problem. *Psychol. Forsch.*, 1931, 15, 1-144.

Dethier, V. G. Microscopic brains. *Science*, 1964, 143, 1138-1145.

Dethier, V. G. Insects and the concept of motivation. In: D. Levine (Ed.), *Nebraska symposium on motivation*, Lincoln, Nebr.: Nebraska Univ. Press, 1966, 105-136.

Deutsch, J. A. The inadequacy of the Hullian derivations of reasoning and latent learning. *Psychol. Rev.*, 1956, 63, 389-399.

Deutsch, J. A. *The structural basis of behavior.* Chicago: Univ. Chicago Press, 1960.

Diggory, J. C. *Self-evaluation: concepts and studies.* N.Y.: Wiley, 1966.

Dollard, J., Doob, L. W., Miller, N. E., Mowrer, O. H., and Sears, R. R. *Frustration and aggression.* New Haven, Conn.: Yale Univ. Press, 1939.

Duffy, E. The concept of energy mobilization. *Psychol. Rev.*, 1951, 58, 30-40.

Edwards, W. The theory of decision making. *Psychol. Bull.*, 1954, 51, 380-417.

Edwards, W. Behavioral decision theory. *Annu. Rev. Psychol.*, 1961, 12, 473-498.

Edwards, W. Utility, subjective probability, their interaction, and variance preferences. *J. Confl. Resol.*, 1962, 6, 42-51.

Ellis, N. R., and Pryer, M. W. Primary versus secondary reinforcement in simple discrimination learning of mental defectives. *Psychol. Repts.*, 1958, 4, 67-70.

Epstein, A. N., and Teitelbaum, P. Regulation of food intake in the absence of taste, smell, and other oropharyngeal sensations. *J. comp. physiol. Psychol.*, 1961, 55, 753-759.

Estes, W. K. Stimulus-response theory of drive. In: M. R. Jones (Ed.), *Nebraska symposium on motivation.* Lincoln, Nebr.: Nebraska Univ. Press, 1958, pp. 35-69.

Fajans, S. Die Bedeutung der Entfernung für die Stärke eines Aufforderungscharakters beim Säugling und Kleinkind. *Psychol. Forsch.*, 1933, 17, 215-267.

Freud, S. Psychopathology of everyday life. In: A. A. Brill (Trans. and Ed.), *The basic writings of Sigmund Freud.* N.Y.: Modern Library, 1938.

Gallistel, C. R. Electrical self-stimulation and its theoretical implications. *Psychol. Bull.*, 1964, 61, 23-34.

Gallistel, C. R. Intracranial stimulation and natural reward: differential effects of trial spacing. *Psychon. Sci.*, 1967, 9, 167-168.

Garcia, J., and Koelling, R. A. Relation of cue to consequence in avoidance learning. *Psychon. Sci.*, 1966, 4, 123-124.

Goffman, E. *Interaction ritual: Essays on face-to-face behavior*. Garden City, N.Y.: Doubleday, 1967.

Gollin, E. S., and Savoy, P. Fading and conditional discrimination in children. *J. exp. Anal. Behav.*, 1968, 11, 443-451.

Goodrich, K. P. Experimental analysis of response slope and latency as criteria for characterizing voluntary and nonvoluntary responses in eyeblink conditioning. *Psychol. Monogr.*, 1966, 80, No. 14 (Whole No. 622).

Greenblatt, M. H. The "legal" value of π, and some related mathematical anomalies. *Amer. Scientist*, 1965, 53, 427A-432A.

Griggs, R. C., and Stunkard, A. The interpretation of gastric motility. II. Sensitivity and bias in the perception of gastric motility. *Arch. gen. Psychiatr.*, 1964, 11, 82-89.

Hart, H. L. A. *Punishment and responsibility. Essays in the philosophy of law*. New York and London: Oxford Univ. Press, 1968.

Hebb, D. O. *The organization of behavior. A neuropsychological theory*. N.Y.: Wiley, 1949.

Hess, E. H. Natural preferences of chicks and ducklings for objects of different colors. *Psychol. Rep.*, 1956, 2, 477-483.

Hoebel, B. G., and Teitelbaum, P. Hypothalamic control of feeding and self-stimulation. *Science*, 1962, 135, 375-377.

Hull, C. L. The goal gradient hypothesis and maze learning. *Psychol. Rev.*, 1932, 39, 25-43.

Hull, C. L. Differential habituation to internal stimuli in the albino rat. *J. comp. Psychol.*, 1933, 16, 255-273.

Hull, C. L. *Principles of behavior: An introduction to behavior theory*. N.Y.: Appleton-Century, 1943.

Hull, C. L. *A behavior system*. New Haven: Yale Univ. Press, 1952.

Irwin, F. W. The concept of volition in experimental psychology. In: F. P. Clarke and M. C. Nahm (Eds.), *Philosophical essays in honor of Edgard Arthur Singer, Jr.* Phila.: Univ. Pennsylvania Press, 1942, pp. 115-137.

Irwin, F. W. An analysis of the concepts of *discrimination* and *preference*. *Amer. J. Psychol.*, 1958, 71, 152-163.

Irwin, F. W. On desire, aversion, and the affective zero. *Psychol. Rev.*, 1961, 68, 293-300.

Irwin, F. W. Criteria of expectancy. *Psychol. Rev.*, 1966, 73, 327-334.

Irwin, F. W., and Graae, C. N. Tests of the discontinuity hypothesis of the effects of independent outcome values upon bets. *J. exp. Psychol.*, 1968, 76, 444-449.

Irwin, F. W., Orchinik, C. W., and Weiss, J. Studies in object-preferences: The effect of temporal proximity upon adults' preferences. *Amer. J. Psychol.*, 1946, 59, 458-462.

Irwin, F. W., and Snodgrass, J. G. Effects of independent and dependent outcome values upon bets. *J. exp. Psychol.*, 1966, 71, 282-285.

Irwin, F. W., and Tolkmitt, F. Buying insurance in an urn-scheme experiment. *Psychon. Sci.*, 1968, 12, 287-288.

James, W. *Principles of psychology*. N.Y.: Holt, 1890.

Jenkins, J. J., and Hanratty, J. A. Drive intensity discrimination in the albino rat. *J.*

comp. physiol. Psychol., 1949, 42, 228-232.

Karsten, A. Psychische Sättigung. *Psychol. Forsch.*, 1927, 10, 142-254.

Katkin, E. S., and Murray, E. N. Instrumental conditioning of autonomically mediated behavior: theoretical and methodological issues. *Psychol. Bull.*, 1968, 70, 52-68.

Kendler, H. H. The influence of simultaneous hunger and thirst drives upon the learning of two opposed spatial responses of the white rat. *J. exp. Psychol.*, 1946, 36, 212-220.

Keys, A., Brozek, J., Henschel, A., Mickelsen, O., and Taylor, H. L. *The biology of human starvation*. Minneapolis: Univ. of Minnesota Press, 1950.

Kimble, G. A. *Hilgard and Marquis' Conditioning and learning*. N.Y.: Appleton-Century-Crofts, 1961.

Kimble, G. A., and Perlmuter, L. C. The problem of volition. *Psychol. Rev.*, 1970, 77, 361-384.

Labov, W. The social motivation of a sound change. *Word*, 1963, 19, 273-309.

Lambert, W. W., and Solomon, R. L. Extinction of a running response as a function of distance of block point from the goal. *J. comp. physiol. Psychol.*, 1952, 45, 269-279.

Lashley, K. S. The mechanism of vision. XV. Preliminary studies of the rat's capacity for detail vision. *J. gen. Psychol.*, 1938, 18, 123-193.

Leeper, R. The role of motivation in learning: a study of the phenomenon of differential motivational control of the utilization of habits. *J. genet. Psychol.*, 1935, 46, 3-40.

Leeper, R. W. A motivational theory of emotion to replace emotion as disorganized response. *Psychol. Rev.*, 1948, 55, 5-21.

Lewin, K., Dembo, T., Festinger, L., and Sears, P. S. Level of aspiration. In: J. McV. Hunt (Ed.), *Personality and the behavior disorders*. N.Y.: Ronald Press, 1944, Vol. I, pp. 333-378.

Lindsley, D. B. Emotion. In: S. S. Stevens (Ed.), *Handbook of experimental psychology*. N.Y.: Wiley, 1951, pp. 473-516.

Logan, F. A. A micromolar approach to behavior theory. *Psychol. Rev.*, 1956, 63, 63-73.

Logan, F. A. *Incentive: how the conditions of reinforcement affect the performance of rats*. New Haven: Yale Univ. Press, 1960.

Logan, F. A. Continuously negatively correlated amount of reinforcement. *J. comp. physiol. Psychol.*, 1966, 62, 31-34.

Lorenz, K. *On agression*. N.Y.: Bantam Books, 1969.

Lovejoy, E. *Attention in discrimination learning: a point of view and a theory*. San Francisco: Holden-Day, 1968.

Luce, R. D., and Raiffa, H. *Games and decisions*. N.Y.: Wiley, 1957.

Luce, R. D., and Suppes, P. Preference, utility, and subjective probability. In: R. D. Luce, R. R. Bush, and E. Galanter (Eds.), *Handbook of mathematical psychology*. N.Y.: Wiley, 1965, Vol. 3, Ch. 19, pp. 249-410.

MacCorquodale, K., and Meehl, P. E. Preliminary suggestions as to a formalization of expectancy theory. *Psychol. Rev.*, 1953, 60, 55-63.

Maier, N. R. F. *Frustration. The study of behavior without a goal*. N.Y.: McGraw-Hill, 1949.

Malmo, R. B. Activation: a neuropsychological dimension. *Psychol. Rev.*, 1959, 66, 367-386.

Margules, D. L., and Olds, J. Identical "feeding" and "rewarding" systems in the lateral hypothalamus of rats. *Science*, 1962, 135, 374-375.

Marks, R. W. The effect of probability, desirability, and "privilege" on the stated expectations of children. *J. Person.*, 1951, 19, 332-351.

Marsh, G. Effect of overtraining on reversal and nonreversal shifts in nursery school children. *Child Develpm.*, 1964, 35, 1367-1372.

McClelland, D. C., Atkinson, J. W., Clark, R. A., and Lowell, E. L. *The achievement motive.* N.Y.: Appleton-Century-Crofts, 1953.

McDougall, W. *An introduction to social psychology.* (15th ed.) Boston: J. W. Luce, 1923.

Mendelson, J. Lateral hypothalamic stimulation in satiated rats: the rewarding effects of self-induced drinking. *Science*, 1967, 157, 1077-1079.

Mendelson, J., and Chorover, S. L. Lateral hypothalamic stimulation in satiated rats: T-maze learning for food. *Science*, 1965, 149, 559-561.

Meyer, D. R. The stability of human gustatory sensitivity during changes in time of food deprivation. *J. comp. physiol. Psychol.*, 1952, 45, 373-376.

Miller, G. A., Galanter, E., and Pribram, K. H. *Plans and the structure of behavior.* N.Y.: Holt, 1960.

Miller, J. G. *Unconsciousness.* N.Y.: Wiley, 1942.

Miller, N. E. Experimental studies of conflict. In: J. McV Hunt (Ed.), *Personality and the behavior disorders.* N.Y.: Ronald Press, 1944, Vol. I, pp. 431-465.

Miller, N. E. Fear as an acquirable drive: I. Fear as motivation and fear-reduction as reinforcement in the learning of new responses. *J. exp. Psychol.*, 1948, 38, 89-101.

Miller, N. E. Some reflections on the law of effect produce a new alternative to drive reduction. In: M. R. Jones (Ed.), *Nebraska symposium on motivation*, Lincoln, Nebr.: Nebraska Univ. Press, 1963, 65-112.

Miller, N. E. Learning of visceral and glandular responses. *Science*, 1969, 163, 434-445.

Miller, N. E., and DiCara, L. Instrumental learning of heart rate changes in curarized rats: shaping, and specificity to discriminative stimulus. *J. comp. physiol. Psychol.*, 1967, 63, 12-19.

Miller, N. E., and Kessen, M. L. Reward effects of food via stomach fistula compared with those of food via mouth. *J. comp. physiol. Psychol.*, 1952, 45, 555-564.

Mischel, W., Grusec, J., and Masters, J. C. Effects of expected delay time on the subjective value of rewards and punishments. *J. Person. soc. Psychol.*, 1969, 11, 363-373.

Myer, J. S., and White, R. T. Aggressive motivation in the rat. *Animal Behav.*, 1965, 13, 430-433.

Norman, M. F. An approach to free-responding on schedules that prescribe reinforcement probability as a function of interresponse time. *J. math. Psychol.*, 1966, 3, 235-268.

Osgood, C. E. *Method and theory in experimental psychology.* N.Y.: Oxford Univ. Press, 1953.

Peterson, N. Control of behavior by presentation of an imprinted stimulus. *Science*, 1960, 132, 1395-1396.

Pfaffmann, C., and Bare, J. K. Gustatory nerve discharges in normal and adrenalectomized rats. *J. comp. physiol. Psychol.*, 1950, 43, 320-324.

Poulton, E. C. Tracking behavior. In: E. A. Bilodeau (Ed.), *Acquisition of skill.* N.Y.: Academic Press, 1966, pp. 361-410.

Premack, D. Reinforcement theory. In: D. Levine (Ed.), *Nebraska symposium on motivation.* Lincoln, Nebr.: Univ. Nebraska Press, 1965, pp. 123-180.

Renner, K. E. Conflict resolution and the process of temporal integration. *Psychol. Rep.*, 1964, 15, 423-438.

Renner, K. E. Temporal integration: relative value of rewards and punishments as a function of their temporal distance from the response. *J. exp. Psychol.*, 1966, 71, 902-907.

Renner, K. E. Temporal integration: an incentive approach to conflict resolution. In: B. A. Maher (Ed.), *Progress in experimental personality research.* N.Y.: Academic Press, 1967, Vol. 4, pp. 127-177.

Rescorla, R. A., and Solomon, R. L. Two-process learning theory: relationships between Pavlovian conditioning and instrumental learning. *Psychol. Rev.*, 1967, 74, 151-182.

Roberts, W. W., and Carey, R. J. Rewarding effect of performance of gnawing aroused by hypothalamic stimulation in the rat. *J. comp. physiol. Psychol.*, 1965, 59, 317-324.

Rodgers, W., and Rozin, P. Novel food preferences in thiamine-deficient rats. *J. comp. physiol. Psychol.*, 1966, 61, 1-4.

Rose, M. Personal communication. 1968.

Rozin, P. Specific aversions as a component of specific hungers. *J. comp. physiol. Psychol.*, 1967, 64, 237-242.

Rozin, P., and Rodgers, W. Novel-diet preferences in vitamin-deficient rats and rats recovered from vitamin deficiency. *J. comp. physiol. Psychol.*, 1967, 63, 421-428.

Schachter, S. Obesity and eating. *Science*, 1968, 161, 751-756.

Schachter, S., and Singer. J. E. Cognitive, social, and physiological determinants of emotional state. *Psychol. Rev.*, 1962, 69, 379-399.

Sheffield, F. D., Roby, T. B., and Campbell, B. A. Drive reduction versus consummatory behavior as determinants of reinforcement. *J. comp. physiol. Psychol.*, 1954, 47, 349-354.

Shimp, C. P. Optimal behavior in free-operant experiments. *Psychol. Rev.*, 1969, 76, 97-112.

Singer, E. A., Jr. Royce on love and loyalty. In: *Modern thinkers and present problems.* N.Y.: Henry Holt, 1923, pp. 283-299.

Skinner, B. F. *The behavior of organisms: an experimental approach.* N.Y.: Appleton-Century, 1938.

Solomon, R. L., and Brush, E. S. Experimentally derived conceptions of anxiety and aversion. In: M. R. Jones (Ed.), *Nebraska symposium on motivation.* Lincoln, Nebr.: Univ. Nebraska Press, 1956, pp. 212-305.

Spence, K. W. The nature of discrimination learning in animals. *Psychol. Rev.*, 1936, 43, 427-449.

Spragg, S. D. S. Morphine addiction in chimpanzees. *Comp. Psychol. Monogr.*, 1940, 15, No. 7.

Stevenson, H. W. Discrimination learning. In: N. R. Ellis (Ed.), *Handbook of mental deficiency: psychological theory and research.* N.Y.: McGraw-Hill, 1963.

Stunkard, A., and Koch, C. The interpretation of gastric motility. I. Apparent bias in the reports of hunger by obese persons. *Arch. gen. Psychiatr.*, 1964, 11, 74-82.

Stutz, R. M., Butcher, R. E., and Rossi, R. Stimulus properties of reinforcing brain shock. *Science*, 1969, 163, 1081-1082.

Tenen, S. S., and Miller, N. E. Strength of electrical stimulation of lateral hypothalamus, food deprivation, and tolerance for quinine in food. *J. comp. physiol. Psychol.*, 1964, 58, 55-62.

Terrace, H. S. Discrimination learning with and without "errors." *J. exp. Anal. Behav.*, 1963, 6, 1-27.

Terrace, H. S. Discrimination learning and inhibition. *Science*, 1966, 154, 1677-1680.

Thistlethwaite, D. A critical review of latent learning and related experiments. *Psychol. Bull.*, 1951, 48, 97-129.

Thompson, T. I. Visual reinforcement in Siamese fighting fish. *Science*, 1963, 141, 55-57.

Tinbergen, N. *The study of instinct.* Oxford: Oxford Univ. Press, 1951.

Tolman, E. C. *Purposive behavior in animals and men.* N.Y.: Century, 1932.

Tolman, E. C. Principles of purposive behavior. In: S. Koch (Ed.), *Psychology: a study of a science.* N.Y.: McGraw-Hill, 1959, Vol. 2, 92-157.

Tolman, E. C., and Gleitman, H. Studies in learning and motivation: I. Equal reinforcements in both end-boxes, followed by shock in one end-box. *J. exp. Psychol.*, 1949, 39, 810-819.

Trowill, J. A., Panksepp, J., and Gandelman, R. An incentive model of rewarding brain stimulation. *Psychol. Rev.*, 1969, 76, 264-281.

Turner, L. H., and Solomon, R. L. Human traumatic avoidance learning: Theory and experiments on the operant-respondent distinction and failures to learn. *Psychol. Monogr.*, 1962, 76, No. 40 (Whole No. 559).

Tversky, A. Intransitivity of preferences. *Psychol. Rev.*, 1969, 76, 31-48.

Valenstein, E. S., Cox, V. C., and Kakolewski, J. W. Reexamination of the role of the hypothalamus in motivation. *Psychol. Rev.*, 1970, 77, 16-31.

Watson, J. B. *Psychology from the standpoint of a behaviorist.* Phila.: Lippincott, 1924.

Webb, W. B. Drive stimuli as cues. *Psychol. Rep.*, 1955, 1, 287-298.

Williams, D. R., and Williams, H. Auto-maintenance in the pigeon: sustained pecking despite contingent nonreinforcement. *J. exp. Anal. Behav.*, 1969, 12, 511-520.

Wilson, W. A., Jr. The role of learning, perception, and reward in monkeys' choice of food. *Amer. J. Psychol.*, 1959, 72, 560-565.

Wolfe, J. B. Effectiveness of token-rewards for chimpanzees. *Comp. Psychol. Monogr.*, 1936, 12, No. 5.

Yensen, R. Some factors affecting taste sensitivity in man. *Quart. J. exp. Psychol.*, 1959, 11, 221-248.

Young, P. T. *Motivation of behavior.* N.Y.: Wiley, 1936.

Young, P. T. The experimental analysis of appetite. *Psychol. Bull.*, 1941, 38, 129-164.

Young, P. T. The role of affective processes in learning and motivation. *Psychol. Rev.*, 1959, 66, 104-125.

Young, P. T. *Motivation and emotion. A survey of the determinants of human and animal activity.* N.Y.: Wiley, 1961.

Index of Names

Index of Subjects

Act (*cont.*)

Probability *(cont.)*

expectancy and, 66-67, 150
subjective, 150
Problem-solving, 84
Processes, 106
Projective methods, 142
Psychoanalysis, 96
Psychologist's fallacy, 143-144
Psychology
history and, 20
physiological, 107, 110,
172-174
Psychophysics, catch trial, 16
Punishments, 20
Purpose of act, 11, 19, 79

Quantitative properties of acts *(See*
Act, quantitative prop-
erties of.)
Quinine acceptability, 132

Random order, 43, 112, 128, 153
Rank order, 48, 54, 56
Rate *(See* Act, quantitative
properties of.)
Reaction time, 84
Recall, act of, 17
Reduction, 107
Reflex, 32, 38, 43, 81, 82, 83, 94,
105
conditioned, 81, 83-84, 94,
106, 168, 175
Reflexivity *(See* Relation.)
Refraining from act *(See* Act, of
abstention.)
Reinforcement, 105, 106, 138
by consummatory acts,
168-170
drive-reduction and, 134-135,
136
Premack's theory of, 176-177
secondary, 168
Reinforcement theory, 73, 176-177
Rejected act, 79, 82-83
Relation
asymmetric, 41, 46-48, 56, 68
binary, 46, 50, 56
intransitive, 57
irreflexive, 46-48, 56, 68

nontransitive, 51-54, 54-55, 56
reflexive, 50
symmetric, 42, 51
three-term, 66
transitive, 46-48, 51, 52, 54,
56, 57, 68, 104, 150
(See also Preference, logical
properties of; Indifference,
logical properties of.)
Response
act and, 18, 105
bias, 33 *(See also* Bias.)
differential *(See* Differential
response.)
strength of *(See* Act, quantitative properties of.)
Response, goal, 71-72, 123
Responsibility, 166
Reticular formation, 173
Reversal learning *(See* Act-outcome
expectancy, empirical criteria of; Discrimination;
Preference, empirical criteria of.)
Reversal of preference, 72-73
Rewards, 20
Rule, diagnostic *(See* Diagnostic
rule.)

SAO system
characterized, 4, 103-110
cognition in, 104, 109, 139,
156
compared with other systems,
104-106
decision and, 153
decision theory and, 109, 150,
156
diagrammed, Figs. 1.1, 8.1
discrimination and preference
in, 41-42
drive discrimination and,
111-112
vs. drive theory, 134-137
emotion and, 173-174
errorless discrimination learning and, 97-99
illustrated, 3-12